DO YOU HAVE THE

Courage to Be You?

A Guide to Discover Your Unique Identity and World-changing Destiny!

✤ 10ᵀᴴ ANNIVERSARY EDITION ✤

Jenny Williamson

What People Are Saying

"People who work with human trafficking victims, I call courageous—Jenny Williamson is one of those people. This book details her journey to helping young girls who have been rescued from sex trafficking. But it is more. This book is about you and me finding the courage to be and do all God created us to. Read it! You'll be encouraged and challenged."

—Jeremy Affeldt

Former Pitcher & World Series Champion, San Francisco Giants

. . . . .

"Jenny and her tireless team see the human being who has been brutally exploited and set about to nourish her young soul back into health and possibility. They give a girl a chance to make the courageous choice to run away from her trafficker because there will be a loving circle of arms to fall into."

—Mira Sorvino

Academy Award-winning Actress, United Nations Goodwill Ambassador to Combat Human Trafficking

. . . . .

"As a fellow abolitionist, it is my privilege to join hands with Jenny and Courage Worldwide. Many people do not realize that sex trafficking is happening in the United States. I'm honored to help shine a spotlight on the problem and give people a chance to be a part of the solution."

—Natalie Grant

Grammy-nominated, five-time GMA Dove Award Winner for Female Vocalist of the Year, Human Trafficking Abolitionist

. . . . .

"Jenny Williamson is a one-woman wrecking crew! She lives the message of this book and proves what you can do if you have the courage to be YOU!"

—Reggie McNeal

Best-selling Author, *Get Off Your Donkey! Help Somebody and Help Yourself*

. . . . .

"Life, as we all know, can be hard, and with that comes bitterness and pain. Often without even knowing it, we can become jaded, disguising cynicism as maturity, and somehow, down the line, we forget how to dream. My hope is that this book will do the same for you as it has done for me. Stirring you on to shake off any doubt that you were made for incredible things. We get one shot to tell a great story, and thanks to Jenny and this book, I am re-inspired and re-ignited to write an incredible one with my life. Like most people after meeting Jenny, I walked away dreaming bigger and believing for even greater things, and just like her, this book will do the same for you."

—Philip LaRue

Award-winning Songwriter and National Recording Artist

. . . . .

"*Do You Have the Courage to Be You?* is the biographical statement of a water walker and giant slayer. Read this book, and Jenny's story will become your story. Jenny knows that Identity precedes Destiny. This book will help you discover, define, and develop the future that you were made for from all eternity. God is on the move! Reading this book will help you join Him in your journey!"

—Dr. John Jackson

President of William Jessup University,
Author of *Grace Ambassadors, Finding Your Place in God's Plan,* and *The Right Choice: Choosing a College and Why It Matters*

. . . . .

"I have had the privilege of working with Jenny Williamson to combat sex trafficking in the Sacramento region for well over a year. I am inspired by her seemingly boundless energy and her passion for rescuing the young victims of sex trafficking who are often forgotten by society. Her ability to rally support—not only for Courage House but also for anti-trafficking efforts at every level—is truly remarkable. In a Congressional hearing last year, every single one of the thirteen witnesses testified that the key to getting girls away from traffickers is providing safe housing with comprehensive services. Jenny is exactly on target in her approach, and I commend her and her visionary team for their diligence in building Courage House. I am honored to celebrate the opening of Courage House as a refuge for vulnerable women and children who have been exposed to unspeakable exploitation. Thank you, Courage Worldwide, for giving hands and feet to your vision!"

—Dan Lungren

Former California Attorney General and U.S. Congressman for California (2011–2013)

. . . . . .

"The opening of Courage Worldwide's Courage Houses will provide young women with a sanctuary from predators who would take advantage of them, give them the resources to escape the streets and provide an atmosphere of compassion and support. I encourage others to replicate this model as we continue the fight to apprehend perpetrators of sex crimes and help these vulnerable young women get off of the streets and out of harm's way."

—Doris O. Matsui

U.S. Congresswoman, California 7th District

. . . . . .

"In working with the young, underage victims of sex trafficking in both delinquency and dependency, I have come to realize that they present difficult issues relative to placement, counseling, recidivism, and education. In talking with Jenny over the past couple of years regarding the creation of Courage House, it became clear to me that not only did she recognize the need for a place that met the needs of these young women, but Jenny was also willing to include the community in shaping Courage House. As I explained to Jenny very early on, Courage House is sorely needed in our community as well as other communities dealing with the unique problem posed by these young victimized girls."

—Honorable Troy L. Nunley

U.S. District Judge, Eastern District of California

. . . . . .

"It is my privilege to play a part in combating the atrocity of human trafficking. The cycle that these young victims often find themselves in provides little hope for a normal existence. The collaborative efforts of law enforcement, prose-cutors, and community-based organizations shed light on this crisis and seek justice for its victims. Courage Worldwide's homes (Courage Houses) break the cycle and gives victims an opportunity for a future. Jenny and her team are an effective and indispensable partner in this fight."

–Scott R. Jones

Former Sacramento County Sheriff

. . . . .

"The rate of recidivism is exceptionally high relative to young victims of domestic sex trafficking. This return to the streets occurs because the girls often have nowhere else to go and were initially runaways from abusive situations. Courage House gives them hope, a place to recover and realize the true meaning of 'home.' Courage House gives those of us in law enforce-ment hope for recovery of those we rescue and optimism they won't return to life on the streets."

–Mike Rayfield

Retired Supervisory Special Agent, Violent Crimes Squad, FBI Sacramento

. . . . .

"Courage House is a unique and specially designed program for our victims. It offers a combination of a safe home, specialized treatment, education and training, and, most important of all, the promise of a future free from the past. Courage House is truly an opportunity for these children to chart a new course and find the courage to be the person they were meant to be. Congrat-ulations to Jenny and the Courage House team of volunteers and to the faith community that reached out and embraced a group of children whose needs go unseen under the cover of darkness."

–Carol S. Chrisman

Referee of the Sacramento County Juvenile Court

. . . . .

"Many of us look at the atrocities of our world and say, 'How horrible,' but occasionally some brave soul says, 'How can I help bring an end to this?' Think of William Wilberforce, Martin Luther King Jr., and Mother Teresa. Jenny Williamson is such a brave soul, and Courage Worldwide is a long-overdue answer to the problem of human trafficking. I am honored to be a friend and supporter of this tremendous ministry."

—Dr. Rick Stedman

Founding Pastor, Adventure Christian Church,
Rocklin, California

. . . . .

"Jenny has a way of sifting through the noise or confusion associated with feelings to identify one's priorities and values. She is a great listener who helps boil priorities down into a specific action plan. She does this in her own life and encourages you to do the same regardless of the external pressure or noise to do something else."

—Lynn Bell

Global Account Executive

. . . . .

"Jenny is an amazing speaker. She has a way of instantly grabbing your attention and making you think. Her message of purpose is motivational, and her challenge to be courageous in all areas of life is inspiring. I love her reminder that each of us is here for a specific reason, and if we don't do what we were put here to do, it won't get done. Her encouragement and enthusiasm are contagious! I would highly recommend Jenny for any type of conference, workshop, leadership event, or speaking engagement. She is great!"

—Genny Heikka

Director of Leadership Development, Keynote Speaker,
Author of *Mommy Bliss*

. . . . .

"Jenny is infectious, motivating, and encouraging. She offers a lot of good insight and wisdom during our coaching calls."

—Andy Cude

President, MAC Development

. . . . .

Do You Have the Courage to Be You? A Guide to Discover Your Unique Identity and World-changing Destiny

Copyright © 2015, 2023 by Jenny Williamson

10th Anniversary Edition

Published by Courage Publishing, 12177 Business Park Drive, Suite 2 #313, Truckee, CA, 96161. For more information about this book and the author, visit www.jennytwilliamson.com.

ISBN: Hardcover: 979-8-9889399-0-0
           Paperback: 979-8-9889399-1-7
           Ebook: 979-8-9889399-2-4

Library of Congress Control Number: 2023915255

Cover Design, Interior Design & Typography by:
Linné Garrett | 829 DESIGN | 829Design.com

Editing & Production by:
Jennifer Edwards | jedwardsediting.net

Author Photography by:
Shelby Cude

Due to the sensitive subject matter, names and other identifying information have been altered to protect the privacy of those whose stories and quotes are included in the book.

PRINTED IN THE UNITED STATES OF AMERICA

Dedication

To my husband, Mike, and our sons, Austin,
Michael-Dean, and Ben.

I love you madly. I would give my life, my time,
and my last dime for you. My longing to matter in this
world has never diminished my role as your wife and
mother. Thank you for letting me take this journey of
purpose. I know you have not always understood it.
However, none of you ever asked me to stop.
If you had, I would have said yes.

I pray you each find what I have—the courage
to be and do all God created you to, nothing more,
but absolutely refusing to settle for less.

You are each water walkers, giant slayers,
and history makers.

Always do what you love to do—the thing that makes
your heart sing—and you will change this world.

CONTENTS

FOREWORD

—————————

*elieving my life had a purpose beyond being sold for sex was a dream that was too far-fetched to believe in until I met Jenny Williamson, and she asked me if I had the courage to be me. She relentlessly pursued me with that question. She also told me that before time began, I was created on purpose for a purpose and that I had a water-walking, giant-slaying, history-making destiny. I wanted to believe her, but I was too scared. So Jenny believed in me until I could finally believe in myself.

Every word written on these pages Jenny spoke out loud to me until they became my own. Her words of encouragement, her stories, and her journey detailed throughout this book have become part of my own life. She went so far as to call me "daughter" and invite me into her heart, her life, and her home. It was Jenny and this book that showed me who I was long after everyone else in the house had gone to sleep. Jenny's words destroyed the isolation I felt that comes with not being known, loved, or valued for who I truly was—and who I could be. This book changed my life and my world. I believe it can change yours too. As Jenny—my mom—says, we are all created on purpose for a purpose. It just took me a little time and a lot of courage to believe that was true of me. Now I believe you, too, can find your true identity and destiny within the pages of this book.

Do You Have the Courage to Be You? is more than a book to me. It was and is the heart cry of my mother who said yes to her destiny and, because of that, saved mine. It is the process and story I have lived out and struggled through for the last four years as I have fought to claim my true identity and fulfill my real destiny. This book was and is a roadmap to my future. Without it, and without Jenny and her family, my new family, cheering me on, I would never have had the courage to believe there was more to me or for me. The words in this book convinced me. They also gave me tangible steps and practical things to do to change the lies I so easily believed about myself. When I changed the way I thought, it changed the way I felt about myself, and then I began to make different choices—healthy choices. These choices have propelled me forward into my future. If I had not allowed the truths in this book to move me and change me, I would be dead.

Everything this book did for me, I am convinced, can be done for you. *Nobody is a lost cause.*

I continue to work through the processes contained within these pages, and they continue to shape who I am. I still use the tools Jenny offers. Her stories gave me the courage to write my own story. She convinced me that I can be a water walker, giant slayer, and history maker. Through these pages and through her life, she gave me the courage to be me. I believe this book can do the same for you.

—Liz Williamson
One of Jenny's daughters

ACKNOWLEDGMENTS

I wasn't planning on writing a book. I am a speaker. I find it very easy to express myself face to face, whether with an audience of thousands or in a one-on-one conversation. Writing is hard work! But thanks to a multitude of people who encouraged me to sit down and write, I am now a speaker who also wrote a book. This space is my attempt to thank all of those who gave me encouragement as well as a kick in the butt.

I have a fortune cookie that I have been carrying around in my purse for over ten years. It says, *"Write the book!"*

When I opened it, I laughed out loud and said, *"Okay! Okay! It seems God even speaks through fortune cookies!"* I had been ignoring the encouragement I had received from God's favorite messengers—humans.

Papa Joe Johnson stopped me almost thirteen years ago when I was walking off a stage after speaking at a Courage Conference. He said, *"Jenny, God has pressed upon my heart that you should write the book!"*

Our entire staff at Courage Worldwide also seemed to think there were others who would also be encouraged by my journey and the message I am so passionate about—that each of us has been created on purpose for a purpose. Nina Boatman, Stephanie Midthun, and Melissa Herrmann were a choir singing the same song: *"Write the book!"* Genny Heika and Celeste Reinhart were especially relentless in their encouragement to put on paper what God had put in my heart.

Thank you to the hundreds of women who came to our Courage Conferences. You lined up after each and every one of them, asking, *"Is there a book?"* When I repeatedly replied "no," you asked me to please take the time and write it all down. It took a while, but I finally did just that. Thank you for purchasing a copy for yourself and having me send one to someone you knew needed its message.

Then, years later . . . this gorgeous ten-year-anniversary book is now a reality! Without Jennifer Edwards, this beautiful edition of my book would not have ever been seen by another human being. She, in her most gentle manner, pushed, prodded, and pleaded with me to meet deadlines! She is an extraordinary editor. She makes me sound much better than I talk. It was entirely her idea for this edition, and she enlisted Linné Garrett to design the cover and create the layout, which is stunning, Linné! And now, Jennifer wants me to write a teen edition, so stay tuned! A huge thanks to my daughter-in-law (love), Katie, for reading my words over and over and making them better. Also, thank you to Shelby Cude for taking the author photos that captured my personality and the colors I love. I'm grateful.

To my Creator. You whispered this question, *"Do you have the courage to be you—the you I created?"* on my fortieth birthday, and it literally changed the entire trajectory of my life when I finally said yes. Who knew it would become a book title? (I guess you did!)

To my husband, who believes in me more than I believe in myself . . . you didn't encourage me to write, you just encouraged me to fly! I could not be me without you. Madly.

HEY, YOU!

Did you know you were created specifically on purpose for a purpose? Yes, I am talking about *you*.

Have you ever contemplated that your destiny could change lives or even the world? Did you know people are waiting for you to have the courage to be you—that you being you matters?

Do not feel bad if your answer to these questions is no. I have found that most people do not have a clue as to why they are on this planet. Thoughtfully planned, uniquely molded, and specifically created on purpose for a purpose sounds like a nice concept and much better than being a random cosmic accident. The trouble is that most of us have no idea how to find our specific purpose, even if we believe we have one. We do not see much evidence of people living courageous, purpose-filled lives these days. Well, maybe in the movies we watch or the books we read. Heroes, we call them. Extraordinary individuals. We do not see or believe that we, too, are essential, significant, or necessary to this world. Thus, we never go in search of who we truly are and what we were created to do. Sadly, settling for mediocrity and less than we were created for becomes our default mode. It just seems easier.

I understand.

I felt pitifully ordinary for most of my life. I believed I had no particular recognizable talent. Talkative, hyperactive, loud, and bossy are not descriptions one celebrates but were bestowed upon me. My career prior to going on this journey of purpose consisted of tasks that most anyone could have accomplished. I have been a mom since I was twenty years old. It is a role I treasure. However, no one invited me to be on talk shows to discuss my extraordinary and world-changing parenting skills or comment on our afternoon at the park. Those precious years are now gone, and my three sons are adults making their own mark in this world.

I am not complaining. My life was good. It was just boring. I was cloaked in comfort and choking on mediocrity. I wanted to matter. I longed to make a real difference in this world, in my world, and I wanted to believe there was a specific plan and purpose for *me*. So, near my fortieth birthday, I resolved to find it. Though it took some time, I did just that.

I want to help you do the same.

My journey of purpose and search for meaning has been exciting but more difficult and time-consuming than I now believe was necessary. I wasted precious time asking the wrong questions and leaping in the wrong direction. I did most of it alone, blindly stumbling along an undefined path with no concrete *how-tos* or specific steps. It required a great deal of courage and faith to leave my comfort zones to travel into the unknown in search of my purpose. However, I would do it all over again. Every step has been worth it.

I wrote this book to save you time in discovering and beginning to fulfill your purpose. I believe the tangible, intentional steps I took and the lessons I learned will propel you quickly into your destiny. That is a big deal because someone in the world needs you to be all you were created to be. You see, the world needs you! You were created to be extraordinary. I know my purpose is not yours, but by reading about how I found mine, you might see how God takes someone ordinary and does the extraordinary.

Allow me to start at the end of my story.

We live in a world where children are sold for sex. It is wrong. More than wrong, it is horrendous, despicable, and even loathsome. When I first learned of this evil, I was sitting in church with two of my sons. My mother's heart physically ached, and I cried out loud for these faceless children. When I learned this was happening in my own backyard, I dried my tears and got angry with God for this hideous injustice. I lashed out at Him and demanded *He do something!* Then deep within my heart, I heard Him quietly whisper to me:

Why don't you?

Me? I am just a mom!

Good. That is exactly what these children need.

But I do not have any money.

I will give you all you need.

People will think I am crazy!

So? These are your daughters, and your daughters are being raped, abused, tortured, and sold every single night. Why don't you do something?

Okay, but what?

Build them a home and call them family.

With the argument over, I did just what He said. And I am still doing this over twenty years later. This very ordinary mom made a courageous decision to be who God created her to be so these vulnerable children would have the chance to be and do all they were created to. *By faith.*

I believe God called me to these children to build them homes around the world and call them family so that I can tell them they were created on purpose for a purpose. I am to encourage and help others discover who they are and what they are supposed to be doing.

Which brings me back to you. Who is waiting on *you* to be *you*?

When *you* have the courage to be you—*the you God created*—lives will change! More children will be rescued and restored; the hungry will be fed, the sick will be healed, the lonely befriended, and the brokenhearted comforted. People are praying a prayer waiting on God, and He is waiting on you.

Do you have the courage to be you, the *you* He created?

You do not have to be born courageous or feel brave, you just need to make daily choices that will move you into your water-walking, giant-slaying, history-making destiny! If you read this entire book and take the suggested steps, I am confident you will be filled with a sense of urgency and boldness to do just that.

Yes, you must dedicate time and be determined to make the courageous choices necessary to be and do all you were created to do. I will provide encouragement and *how-tos*. I will be your coach and cheerleader through the pages of this book and the words of my story.

Take courage!

Jenny Williams

Do You Have
the Courage
 to Be You?

There are two me's

inside of me.

The one I am.

And the one I long to be.

The one I am

is familiar and true.

She expects little of me

yet dreams of more, too.

She seems somewhat less

while wanting something more.

But comfort surrounds her soul,

keeping her safe to the core.

Now the other ME that
lives inside of me,

is the opposite for sure.

She plots and plans

her escape from the same.

She longs to do more,

to see more,

to *be* more,

all the while using my name!

The one me and the other
were once the same child.
But as time hurried onward
I lost her somehow.
I gradually began
wanting others to see,
just a mirror, a reflection
of themselves instead of me.

I am not aware
of when the thought
first occurred.
Or when I recognized the truth,
But slowly I heard,
"How did this happen or come to be?
When did you become less,
so much less,
than I designed you to be?"

At first I grew sad,
experienced a terrible ache.
I then began to ponder
all that was at stake.
Another thought surfaced,
as scary as the last,
What if others needed me to be me?
Then I better become *me*—fast!
A heavy sigh I let out,
as I began to pray.

"Lord, grant me the courage,
(on this very day)
to cease to be
more of the same.
But for me to become me
and forever remain."

I then asked a question
of my Father so true,
"What does she look like—
this little girl I once knew?"
"Ah," He said,
"In her, I delight—
let me tell you her secrets
And how to give her life."

"She's as beautiful as a sunset.
An original of mine.
Man's approval does not matter,
as she completes her design.
She sings with the angels,
dances only for my smile.
Laughs with abandon,
knowing she is here
for a short while."

"What are you afraid of?"
My Father asked of me.

"Don't you know by now
your purpose to be?

Lean close while I tell you
what you are longing to know.

I created you only; only so—

that you would be the *me*
I designed you to be."

"Nothing more, my beloved one.

Settling for less cannot be done.

Take my hand and
with courage soar

To the dreams and destiny

I have in store.

Safety and comfort are
not yours to be

But a life lived fully alive
so others can see

that they too were created
on purpose for a purpose

And a great destiny."

PART ONE

Finding Your Identity

Every man and woman is born into the world to do something unique
and something distinctive, and if he or she does not do it,
it will never be done.

—Dr. Benjamin Mays

CHAPTER 1

You Being You Matters

*B*efore time began, you were imagined, planned, and lovingly created on purpose for a purpose—a specific, unique, and one-of-a-kind purpose for you and you alone. Deposited deep inside of you is everything you need to achieve your purpose in this life. Your purpose will transform lives and change the world. It is imperative that you succeed in discovering and fulfilling your destiny because lives are at stake!

I was shocked when I realized this truth applied to me:

"I would literally be dead if you had said 'no' to God. If you had quit, I would not be here. Thank you for giving me a safe place to call home and a family."

A twenty-three-year-old young woman said these words to me after she left the world of sex trafficking. Her biological parents sold her for the purpose of pornography, torture, and sex when she was six years old. Trapped in slavery and owned by a series of men, she was trafficked around the world for the pleasure of one and the profit of another. When her hopes of rescue went unanswered, she began to pray that God would let her die. He did not honor this prayer. Despite her past and pain, He had good plans for her. Ones that involved my family and me.

Realizing how my life, choices, and purpose could impact another was life-changing. News flash! The Creator of the universe also has life-changing plans for you—plans that affect you and others.

Waiting for You to Become You

I am filled with the urgency for you to believe this life-changing truth. When you are being you—the *you* God created you to be—lives *will be* changed, history *will be* made, and prayers *will be* answered. The world is waiting for you to become you.

Have you ever contemplated your own uniqueness or dared to believe there is something distinctive that you alone were created to do? If you do not dream it, create it, write it, tell it, sing it, or build it, *it* will never be done. Could history or lives really be at stake?

Yes!

Let yourself become pregnant with that possibility. Let these words sink deep within you to the place where your mind and logic cannot interrupt. Allow yourself the divine luxury of believing, for just a moment, that before time began, you were set apart for something great.

Before there was a moose or a mountaintop, an ocean or an otter, a waterfall or walrus; before there were stars in the sky or lightning bugs in the dark, before there was a hippopotamus playing in the mud or a lion roaming the African plains, the Creator of the universe imagined you.

He planned you and deliberately designed you for a specific, incredible, unique purpose.

Right here. Right now.

Imagine your Creator, a painter standing before an enormous blank canvas. You are the canvas. With meticulous strokes, He carefully considers the unique plans He has designed for you as He chooses your eye color, personality, IQ, and everything else about you. The sound of your laughter, the size of your feet, your aptitudes and abilities, and your weakness and vulnerabilities are all part of your design with your distinct purpose in mind. Your birth date and location were strategically determined to optimize your arrival and success. During your creative process, dreams and desires were deposited deep inside of you that, when activated, will lead you to your purpose and destiny.

The thought that went into creating you is inconceivable and mind-boggling. You are a unique masterpiece. All of creation is holding its breath in eager anticipation waiting for you to become you. This fact should move you, expand you, and enlarge your view of yourself! Embrace that you are truly one of a kind and not just some random accident. What has been planned for you and only you will astound you. Just wait!

Created on Purpose

When you play *small*, it benefits no one. You being *less than you* accomplishes nothing. *You were created on purpose for a purpose.* Choose to believe it! Allow that phrase to penetrate your heart. Shove your insecurities aside and embrace that your Creator intends to display His splendor in you. Shining bright is your destiny. Your brightness points back to your Creator.

These truths transformed my life and still propel me out of bed every morning. They override my insecurities and fears. Although life-altering and highly addictive, figuring out who you are and why you are here is not easy. Quite honestly, it is incredibly difficult and very scary because it forces us to leave our well-crafted comfort zones for the unknown, the secure for the insecure, and the possible for the impossible. It requires courage to be and do all we were created for.

For a long time, I believed courage was a personality trait—one I was *not* born with! I am not one to pursue adrenaline-producing adventures or activities, and I never feel the least bit deprived by that. I prefer activities that produce feelings of comfort, safety, and security. Sunday afternoon naps are high on that list, as is reading a good book by a warm fireplace, taking a hot bubble bath, and drinking a glass of California red wine made by a trusted and familiar winemaker. I like to go to the same places, eat the same foods, and hang out with the same people. I am an expert at avoiding surprises and anything that could possibly evoke fear or uncertainty, such as trading stocks, 100 percent commission sales jobs, vacations with strangers, new restaurants, or starting a nonprofit organization!

I want my feet to be on solid ground at all times, and I want to know *exactly* what will happen at least five years in advance. As you can imagine, flying through the jungle on a zip line, bungee jumping off a bridge, or parachuting from a small twin-engine airplane is not on my bucket list.

For those of you who do these things regularly, you may find the journey to a courageous, purpose-filled life easy. The rest of us who are bravery-challenged must take courage to live the powerful, purpose-filled life we were created for.

Choose Courage

Taking courage is something we can all do, an intentional decision we can all make despite the fear we all experience. I made this discovery late in my life. I did not learn this growing up in Jackson, Mississippi, which at the time resembled Mayberry, USA. My family who loved me never encouraged me to embark on a path requiring courage. My teachers at school did not encourage risk. I did not hear it preached from the pulpit at the church I attended every Sunday of my life. I personally did not know anyone who was boldly pursuing a destiny that required a vast amount of courage! Everyone I knew was just trying to be good, pay their bills, keep their kids safe, go on a vacation once a year, and retire as early as possible.

The messages I received for most of my life, whether covert or overt, were *do not take risks, stay safe,* and *be good.* Based on how often I heard, "Go to college, get a job, get married, and have kids," I assumed *that* was my destiny for many years.

But as I approached my fortieth birthday, I became restless. Unsettled. Shaken out of my comfort zone, I was asked a question that challenged me and ultimately transformed my life:

"Do you have the courage to be you—the you I created?"

That question came as an answer to a prayer I was praying. It not only scared me but intrigued me.

Me? Why would it take courage to be me?

That provocative question seared my soul for weeks and months and tempted me into wanting more. Daily, it whispered, creating a restlessness inside me that began to ruin me for the ordinary existence I had settled for. An urgency and passion had been planted inside me to discover who I was and what I was supposed to be doing. I longed to know the *me* I was created to be. I wanted to discover if there really was something I was created to do that no one else could do. I needed to make a difference in this world—my world.

What about you? Are you *comfortable?* Are you settling for less than you were created for—mediocrity?

I pray my words will ignite a spark of longing and desperation in you to begin a journey of discovering who you are and what you are here on this planet for. I pray this book will encourage you and propel you into taking the necessary steps required to fulfill your own water-walking, giant-slaying, history-making destiny. However, I must warn you, destinies of this kind . . .

. . . are not safe,

. . . will make you look crazy,

. . . require that you often say, "I don't know,"

. . . will cause you to spend time alone,

. . . and will scare you to death.

It is a journey walked in wild abandon. Steps of faith, not steps of self-reliance, are required.

The Journey to You!

The premise of this entire book is that you have a Creator who designed you. God created you for a destiny too big to imagine or carry out yourself. That means He alone has all the answers to your questions about you and your purpose. The journey starts with Him, not an abstract, theoretical, cliché version of Him, but one that includes Him as an interactive participant in the process. It has nothing to do with religion but with a relationship with Him. You must consult your Creator.

If talking to God and expecting an answer is new or strange, that's okay. It was for me too. I suggest grabbing a journal to record your progress. It helped me so much! You might get a copy of the workbook I wrote to accompany this book, *Uniquely You! A Faith-Driven Journey to Your True Identity and Water-Walking, Giant-Slaying, History-Making Destiny.*

Write down your thoughts and questions about your identity and purpose, then record any ideas that occur to you, anything at all. Don't dismiss a thing! Talk to your Creator out loud or write letters to Him in the pages of your journal, just as you would talk to or write a letter to anyone you are in a relationship with. You do not have to use fancy, formal words. You can be blunt and painfully honest about your doubts and even skeptical about the process if that is how you feel. You do not have to believe in God for Him to believe in you. What do you lose by entertaining the thought that the God of all creation designed you and has a grand purpose for you? It is certainly much better than believing you are of no consequence, just a cosmic accident of no significance.

I admit that hearing God's voice or even my own heart is often difficult. Our world and our lives are so noisy. I hear better outside in wide-open spaces far from noise, buildings, and people. Nature is a beautiful church. You may prefer sitting still in a special place within your home. Listening to music may help you contemplate your existence and feel your heart and His voice. There is no right or wrong way to communicate with God. Just talk. Then *listen* for His still, small voice and your own.

Finding the true *you* and what you were created to do is an amazing adventure. There are battles to fight, giants to slay, and treasures to uncover. It is a journey where logic is challenged, the ordinary becomes extraordinary, and the impossible becomes possible. It is worth the effort because you and your purpose will change lives, history *will be* made, and prayers *will be* answered. It is what you were created for.

Is your heart racing? Mine is! Let's get started!

CHAPTER 2

Questions of Purpose

*B*efore I realized I lived in a world where children are sold for sex, my life was extremely comfortable and safe. Some would say I had it all. However, it did not satisfy my soul's longing to matter and make a difference in this world. Before my fortieth birthday, I began asking those mid-life questions,

Is this all there is? Why am I here? Do I matter?

Just asking them altered the entire trajectory of my life. I longed to be a part of something bigger than I was, for someone to say their life was better because I breathe, that the world is a better place because I live. I wanted to matter. I wanted to make a difference. I just did not know how.

At some point in your life, if you have not already, you may ask the same existential questions that I did. Even though we may be traveling at different paces, we all end up in the same place, wondering who we are, why we are here, and how to make a difference. This longing is part of our DNA, put inside us by our Creator to ignite our journey of purpose. Mine began in the year 2000. The catalyst for me was my approaching fortieth birthday.

I love birthdays, especially mine, but sometime during the months before my fortieth birthday celebration, I ran smack into a brick wall. I never dreaded a birthday until that one. My mind screamed, and my body confirmed, "My life is half over, and I don't have anything to show for it!"

There was no riveting synopsis when I looked back over the first forty years of my life. It seemed I had lived the first forty years in pure reaction to a whirlwind of circumstances, whipped around by whatever life or chance threw my way. There was nothing purposeful, intentional, or passionate about my life. Though extremely busy, I had not accumulated much in the way of meaningful accomplishments, passionate pursuits, or history-making exploits. This new awareness brought a desperate desire to have all three.

Living on Purpose

After much pre-birthday contemplation, I intensely longed to live a life of purpose. Even though I looked, I could not find tangible resources offering ways to equip, encourage, and empower me to discover and fulfill my destiny. Sure, many wonderful organizations existed to feed the poor, heal the sick, and educate children around the world, but I could not find many devoting their time and resources to helping ordinary people like me find their purpose.

Though I had no road map or clue on how to start, with great intention and enormous conviction, I vowed to live the next forty years of my life vastly different from the first. Still, I had more questions than answers.

What is my purpose? How do I find it? Why am I here?

I asked these questions to no one in particular. I would lay awake during the night, wrestling with them in my mind. No answers or clarity came with the morning, just an uneasy feeling, like one that accompanies a disturbing dream you cannot quite remember. While the nights dragged on, my days seemed to fly by as fast as falling stars. Mirrors confirmed I was aging by the minute. I was sure I was having a mid-life crisis or a nervous breakdown. Exhaustion crept in, along with the knowledge that I would never find the answers to the questions of my soul by myself.

Out of sheer desperation, I made another intentional decision—to seek God for my answers, not myself or other people. After months of restlessness, God seemed to be the obvious source of enlightenment. That was not odd to me since I had believed in Him all my life. I did wonder, though, if He really had my answers. It was time to find out, so I asked my questions to my Creator,

"What am I here for?"

"Why am I on this planet?"

"Do I have a purpose?"

I heard no heavenly answers. I saw no burning bushes. The seas did not part. All I got was silence. Maybe I was wrong.

My fortieth birthday came and went. I was frustrated and wondered if my search was in vain.

Ordinary People, World-changing Feats

During this time of silence and frustration, I began reading Bible stories I remembered from my childhood. I was desperate for answers and thought maybe *this* was the way to break the silence and hear God's voice. I assumed I knew all the stories and their endings. I doubted they would be relevant to my quest. I certainly was wrong. They were relevant—very relevant! I was stunned and inspired by these woefully flawed, often dysfunctional, ordinary human beings who God used to impact and change the world. I knew Noah built a boat and brought the animals in two by two so humanity could be saved, but who knew that a couple of chapters later, he would fall down, passed out drunk! I knew David slayed a giant with a slingshot and a few pebbles, and I knew he later became king. But no one ever told me he had an affair with Bathsheba and killed her husband to cover it up! Still, God called him *a man after His own heart*. I was stunned! What about the woman caught red-handed having an affair? The law at the time said she should die. Instead, she was offered grace, forgiveness, a second chance, and her dignity.

As I read these stories, my doubts evaporated. God spoke to me through their stories. I realized He still wants to use ordinary, messed-up people like me to change the world. I wanted more than anything else to walk on water, slay giants with pebbles, and change history. I wanted the scandalous grace and extravagant love I saw offered over and over again. The small flame of longing was now being stoked into an inferno.

I was encouraged but still restless. My questions without answers felt as if they would explode inside of me. I had to *do* something. I headed to the walking trails near our home and enlisted my dog, Jake, a hyperactive Labrador retriever, to keep me company. I walked for miles each day, talking aloud, asking my questions, and waiting on answers that never came. The solitude was unusual and not very typical for an extrovert like me. I was surprised when I began to enjoy and look forward to these walks. The wide-open spaces seemed to expand my soul, and I grew more comfortable with the silence offered there.

On those walks, I found it wildly liberating to be free of people's opinions and the need to make everyone in my life happy. My family and friends commented on the change in me. Some even took offense. I had found something so precious that I was unwilling to give it up, no matter the cost. I had found peace. Peace in the stillness. Peace in the whispers. Peace walking and talking to God. After a while, I even found peace with my unanswered questions. Like a magnet, I was drawn out there day after day.

Then on one very ordinary day, on a very ordinary walk, the extraordinary happened, and the silence ended. Without any warning or shaking of the earth, I *heard* and even *felt* these words:

Do you have the courage to be you—the you I created?

I immediately stopped walking. Everything around me became still and quiet, even Jake. I looked around. No one was there. Instinctively, I knew the question had not come from me but from my Creator—it was divine. I repeated the words out loud, very slowly.

Do you have the courage to be you?

My first reaction was, "No!" Then I realized that after hours and days and miles on the trail, I'd finally heard an answer. I knew it had come from God, from my heart. He answered my questions . . . with a question. I waited for more whispered words, but none came. The silence returned, but this time it did not frustrate me. I was strangely satisfied and very intrigued by this divine question. I concluded that I must have been asking the wrong question. Instead of asking what my purpose is, I should have been asking, *Who am I?* My persistence in seeking was finally paying off.

My walks became longer after *the question*. I was truly perplexed about why it would take courage to be me. I no longer focused on *what* I was created to do but on *who* I was created to be. There was a profound difference between the two. Evidently, the "me" I was created to be was more important than "what" I was created to do. That was fascinating to me!

A divine unveiling occurred in the days and walks that followed. God unveiled me to me. I would ask Him questions about who I was and what I had become. Then I would remember the child I once was. His answers came in the form of my memories. I had not thought about the child I had been in many years. Now I was prompted to do just that. I could see her; I could even feel her. It seemed she had some of my answers.

When Did I Stop Being Me?

I was a well-loved, extremely happy child. I had incredible confidence and was sure of my place in the world. I loved being first at anything and picked for everything. I treasured being the oldest and big sister to my siblings. I took that role very seriously as I did everything else. I cherished my family. I worked hard to be a good girl and never hurt anyone's feelings.

I loved God and told everyone I met that He loved them too. Believing in a good God was easy when you had good parents. Going to church was my favorite pastime. I was incredibly intuitive. Helping someone gave me great joy. I was caring and responsible. Though an extrovert, being alone was also comfortable for me. I did not require much from other people. Someone said I was an old soul. Being with adults and listening to their conversations was much more fun than hanging out with kids my own age.

I loved to tell people what to do and how to do it. I never understood jokes, but I laughed a lot. I loved those no one else loved. I hated when someone felt left out. At the state fair each year, my dad would win a stuffed animal for me at the basketball throw. After his victory, I was able to choose any prize I wanted. I always picked the ugliest, smallest stuffed animal, the one I was certain no one else would choose. I took them home, bestowing them a regal name and giving them a prominent place on my bed. I slept with them all so no one would feel left out.

At school, I picked friends the same way I picked stuffed animals. I chose the ones no one noticed or ever invited home to play. I picked the kids hurt by others with their hands or words. I became their protector and cheerleader. Actually, I was a cheerleader!

I was extremely loud, active, and full of energy. I did not know how to whisper or sit still. In kindergarten, I got an "F" on my report card in naptime because I talked the entire time. I talked nonstop to anyone who would listen. I even talked to myself. When I spoke, I assumed people, even adults, would value what I had to say and agree with my opinions. I was always stunned when they asked me to be seen and not heard. I was *shhhhhhhed* very often.

I was a tomboy who loved baby dolls. My athletic abilities were well-known in the neighborhood where I grew up. I loved competing with and beating boys in any sport. I threw footballs, hit baseballs, and shot basketballs. I was good at almost every sport I tried—gymnastics, diving, softball, even the high jump. I liked to play on a team, and I loved to win. I was always the captain, and I always followed the rules.

I organized everyone and everything. I made decisions quickly and did not worry about outcomes or failures. I wrote poems, kept diaries, and told stories with great animation. I was a leader looking for someone to follow me. I was comfortable on stage and enjoyed having people watch me. I sang in the choir and danced whenever I could. I had no idea that I did not have a talent for either. It never once occurred to me to question whether I was liked or accepted; I just assumed I was.

These memories of the little girl I once was brought a realization that felt like a kick in the stomach. Somewhere along my life's journey, I stopped being me. These memories made me confront the fact that the woman I had become did not resemble the child I once was.

Why? I wondered. Why?

Turning to my Creator for answers, I asked, *"When did I stop being me?"*

The answer came from another memory that had not occurred to me in thirty years, one I had buried deep in my heart.

I was ten years old. My class had just come in from recess on a hot, humid Mississippi day. We had been playing softball, and as usual, I was the organizer of the game and captain of the team. We won! When we returned to class, I took my seat in the front row. "Jenny," my teacher whispered, "the principal wants to see you in her office." Instantly, fear and dread washed over me. My palms started to sweat, and I felt sick to my stomach. Only bad kids went to the principal's office, and I was a good kid. I inherently knew something was wrong.

As I walked out of the classroom, everyone stared at me, speculating in hushed tones about what I must have done to deserve such a fate. I walked slowly down the hall, my ten-year-old mind wondering the same thing.

I had heard stories from the *bad* kids summoned to the principal's office. Long stays after school, cleaning the blackboards, paddles with holes in them, and having to grab your ankles and bend over were all forms of punishment handed out in the principal's office. Yet I was the teacher's pet, and the teacher's pets did not go there.

Walking to the principal's office in shame was *not* a part of my identity. As I inched down the long hallway, I felt my confidence slipping away; that was a new experience for me. My palms were wringing wet. I kept wiping them on my pants. My mind searched for anything I might have said or done that could warrant this summons.

As I rounded the corner and peeked through the office window, the secretary caught my eye and waved me in. Her smile did nothing to encourage me. I sat in the chair she pointed to. I felt so small. I focused all my attention on my feet, swinging back and forth in nervous anticipation of what was going to happen next.

After what felt like an eternity, I heard my name called rather formally, "Jennifer." No one called me Jennifer except on the first day of school, which I quickly corrected by shouting, "Jenny!" Now I was really scared. I did not correct the principal about my name, I just scooted off the chair and, without looking up, followed her into the room where all the bad kids went. She closed the door.

"Take a seat."

I did, once more staring at the floor. I could not look her in the eye. I felt alone, vulnerable, and unprotected.

She wasted no time with pleasantries and attacked immediately. While I am prone to exaggeration, that is exactly what it was—an attack. "Aren't you the young lady who wants to be a missionary and go around the world telling everyone that God loves them?" she asked.

Her words felt like an accusation. They were so different from the affirmations I was accustomed to receiving when I announced my career choice. I looked up for the first time. I was confused. She had just announced my dream, the not-so-secret desire of my heart. I passionately gave this answer to anyone who asked me what I wanted to be when I grew up. Something was wrong. At ten, I didn't know how to articulate that her tone and words dripped with sarcasm.

The way she asked the question made the desire of my heart sound like a hideous aspiration for evil. Unfamiliar emotions poured into my young psyche: humiliation, shame, and embarrassment. I remember nodding, affirming her question. Though it was the truth, for the first time in my young life, I was now embarrassed to admit it. My dream had never been ridiculed, only validated and applauded. These new feelings caused me to look down and stare at my feet.

She broke the silence with another accusation: "If you love God so much, how could you be so unkind to one of your classmates?" I looked up again, shocked! Unkind? I was never unkind. I guess the confused look on my face caused her to continue. She explained how she watched me being mean to Julia at recess during our softball game. Julia was my friend. We had spent many nights together at sleepovers. She did not have any other friends. Everyone laughed and made fun of her because of her weight—everyone except me.

She continued, "You wouldn't let Julia play in the game. You excluded her."

"No!" I wanted to say. "That wasn't true." However, I remained silent while I remembered what had really happened.

The game had already started, and the teams were chosen when Julia walked up. I would have welcomed her on my team, but she only wanted to bat and did not want to take a turn playing in the outfield. I told her she could not do that because it was against the rules. My dad taught me that. If you want a turn at bat, you must take a turn in the outfield. Therefore, Julia decided not to play.

However, I could not say any of this to my principal. I was taught it was disrespectful to talk back to an adult. I was taught to be good. I chose to be silent. That was not like me either.

A Disturbing Vow

I wanted to run away from the emotions unleashed inside me at ten years old and now upon remembering what happened. I was in unfamiliar territory. This person in authority called my actions, my dream, into question. She bestowed a new and foreign identity upon me—hypocritical, self-righteous, and unkind. Who was I to argue or question her authority? I was just a child. It must be my fault. I must have done something wrong.

My ten-year-old filter was inadequate and not yet equipped to reject the lies pouring into my mind and searing my soul. I learned many things that day—being so passionate and vocal about my dreams was wrong. It was wrong to talk about God. It was wrong to be a leader. It was wrong to play by the rules. But the real lesson I learned at the ripe old age of ten was that it was wrong to be *me*.

In those few minutes behind that closed door, I vowed that I would never again do anything to make me feel what I had felt in that principal's office. I made a vow to stop being myself. It was a vow I would keep for the next thirty years.

I told no one about this incident; I was too embarrassed. I just quit. I quit having an opinion. I quit talking about God. I quit leading and started following. I quit writing and telling stories. I quit being on a stage. I did not want anyone to look at me anymore. I began to question who I was. I lost my confidence in being me because I no longer believed being me was good. I morphed into a chameleon. I became an expert at discovering who and what people wanted or needed me to be. I assimilated and became like everyone else. I did not want to stand out anymore. I stopped trying new things. I stood for nothing. I never said no, which got me into difficult situations, especially with boys, from which I was ill-equipped to extract myself as a young girl and teenager. Because I was terrified of those hideous emotions—shame, embarrassment, and humiliation—I stopped being myself and became someone else for a very *long* time.

As God pulled back the veil of my past, I saw that the woman I had become was a direct result of my silent vow made many years ago as a ten-year-old child. As I grew older, I grew more fearful of those hated emotions, so I continued to reshape myself. In doing so, I did not know I would lose the me I was created to be.

I did not believe my opinion was valuable as an adult, so I waited for others to offer theirs first. I still talked a lot, but only about things that did not matter and were not controversial. I joined whatever my peers were joining so I would be included and not stand out. I wore what everyone else wore, drank what everyone else drank, and carried on meaningless conversations. I compared myself to everyone and became very judgmental of others and myself. I still went to church, but I never shared my faith. I settled for mediocrity, comfort, and security. I traded in my dreams and desires, assuming this would protect me from ever being humiliated again. It did not. I had no idea I was trading in my destiny when I stopped being me.

Now I grasped why I was afraid and could not answer the question, *"Do you have the courage to be you?"* I did not believe there was more for me. Even more profoundly, I did not believe there was more *to* me. I finally realized why I was so scared and why I needed the courage to be me. Deep in the recesses of my soul, where words are not necessary, settling for less was the only thing I knew how to do. I embraced the lifestyle of never believing in or expecting anything extraordinary. I did not know how to believe in myself, much less *be me*. I had embraced an identity that was not mine.

It was as if my Creator pushed a pause button on my destiny. I was having an identity crisis that needed immediate attention. I was not being me, so I had to remove the false, protective identity I had been wearing for years and accept the one that resembled the bold, confident child I once was. Before I could ever walk on water, I had to first learn to be me. I needed to carefully assess who I was before I could figure out what I was supposed to do.

Welcome to Identity Boot Camp

When I set out to undo thirty years of insecurity and false identity, I called this time in my life *identity boot camp*, which proved to be a long process. As I practiced being and believing in myself, I heard a new whisper that gave me all the courage I needed:

"You were created on purpose for a purpose."

These words seared my soul. Revelation dawned—me being me mattered. My identity and destiny were related. They were purposefully intertwined. This declaration felt extraordinarily personal and stirred up a longing inside me that caused all doubts and fear to vanish. Passionately I declared, "Yes! Yes! Yes! I want to be me!" I vowed never again to settle for less than I was created for. That day, I prayed, "Give me the courage to be me."

It is clear to me now that my fortieth birthday was used to ignite a flame of longing in my heart to be me, nothing more but absolutely refusing to settle for anything less. The drama and subsequent meltdown were not parts of a mere mid-life crisis or random event. It was the divine, invisible, loving hand of my Creator wooing me to my true identity and destiny.

Because you picked up this book, maybe you are being wooed to your true identity and unique destiny! Let my question be yours: Do *you* have the courage to be you—the *you* God created?

I pray you'll say yes and then begin your journey of purpose by asking your Creator for clues to your identity and destiny. One of my clues was remembering the little girl I once was. As you read my story, I hope it brought to mind the child you once were. Reflect on who you were when you were younger. Consider your personality and your dreams. What did you love to do? Who did you like to spend time with? Consider if you were an extrovert or an introvert, talkative or quiet. Did you like to read, sing, or draw? Did you have a particular talent? Were you competitive? What were you going to be when you grew up? Why?

All these questions can prompt memories that may be important to uncover your identity and destiny.

Do you now resemble the child you once were? Did you fulfill all your dreams? If so, I am so happy for you! This journey of purpose will go much quicker because you will have less to undo than the rest of us who, for some reason or another, decided that who we were was not such a good idea. When did you stop being you?

Consult your Creator with these questions and see if He gives you any insight into the connection between the child you once were and the adult you have become. There could be clues and connections for your identity and destiny in those memories. You may have made vows like mine that are robbing you of your true identity and world-changing destiny. Take the time to remember.

CHAPTER 3

Your Identity Precedes
Your Destiny

*H*ave you ever wondered where your identity came from? Did your parents, friends, spouse, co-workers, or even a boss bestow an identity upon you that you ultimately embraced? Have you ever considered if this identity is genuinely you or if you've been living out of a false identity?

Who are you, really?

Unfortunately, you cannot do what you were created to do until you know who you were created to be. Your identity precedes your destiny. We all want to know the "what" but run from figuring out the "who." Like me, you may need an identity boot camp.

From the day we arrived in this world, there has been a never-ending supply of people telling us who we are—or rather, who they want us to be. Our society and the media—especially social media—also want a voice in bestowing our identity. They shout that we must be rich, powerful, skinny, smart, and gorgeous to be happy. We must wear designer clothes and drive a sexy, expensive car to the hottest gathering place in town if we are ever to be noticed and "significant." This worldly identity sells everything from iPhones to underwear. It is a very easy lie to buy into when we compare ourselves to others, and has become a competitive sport!

These types of bogus advertisements confirm that we are a society lacking identity. It is a plague on our world. No wonder so many people live lives of quiet desperation and lack of purpose. Who can measure up? Individually and collectively, we have no sense of our unique identity or world-changing destiny. I am especially shocked by people who profess to believe in God yet do not see themselves as valuable, cherished, planned, and loved. Our world screams at us while our Creator whispers to our souls.

The truth is this lack of identity is robbing us all of our destinies.

Understanding Your True Identity

Wasted lives. Unfilled purposes. There is nothing sadder and nothing further from God's plans for humanity and His plans for you. Let's consider who your Creator says you are.

You are a child of God.

If you were raised going to church your entire life, that sentence may not wow you or seem the least bit significant to your identity and destiny. Often mere repetition of a phrase can remove its designed impact and implications. And if you have never heard it or entertained the thought, it may seem like religious jargon and not carry much weight.

While reading this book, I hope you will entertain and contemplate the possibility that you were divinely created by a heavenly Father who loves you. He not only loves you but created you and placed you here in this particular time for a reason and purpose. He calls you beloved. He calls you His own. He adopted you into a loving family much larger than your biological one. There isn't anything you have to do. He has done it all! It is an unmovable, never-changing, irrevocable identity. Who you are is an image of God. He has planted His attributes in you. When you love, He is loving. When you show compassion, He is showing His compassion through you. When you give, He is giving. When you respond, a prayer is being answered. We are God's plan for this world. If we do not realize, internalize, and personalize this identity, we may never believe we can walk on water, slay giants with stones, or change the course of history for all eternity. We may never step into our destiny.

There is so much at stake!

This identity as a child of God guarantees that you know you are loved, planned, and have a place to belong. Your identity does not depend upon the family you were born into or the labels bestowed upon you. Low self-esteem, codependent, addict, overweight, orphan, or any other label you may struggle under is simply that—a label. They are not *who* you are; they are not your identity. Chosen, cherished, and valued are yours to claim. This identity guarantees you success in your destiny. Your adoption changes everything! It did for me, and it certainly did for my grandmother.

Bessie Richards Smith, aka Elizabeth

My grandmother's given name at birth was Bessie Richards Smith. She was born on September 29, 1912, in Hickman, Kentucky, to Willford Lee Smith and Maude Ivy Smith. Willford was twenty-two when he asked Maude's father for her hand in marriage. Maude was fourteen, a common "marrying age" in the South at that time. The young couple married and moved Maude from her hometown of Memphis, Tennessee, to Willford's of Hickman, Kentucky. Hickman is located on the mighty Mississippi River.

Willford found work on a riverboat, and there they settled, raising a family. When Maude was twenty-one and pregnant with my grandmother, her fifth child, Willford unexpectedly died of pneumonia. Suddenly, Maude was alone with four small children to provide for; her family was far away in Tennessee. I cannot imagine how scared she must have been. While I have no detailed account or family stories of this time, we know Maude gave birth to my grandmother and decided to travel back to her family in Memphis alone with four young children and a baby. During her journey home, her oldest daughter, Clara, died of scarlet fever.

I do not know how she kept going. Courage? A sense of purpose? Faith in God? Desperation? Probably all of the above.

However, I do know that when Maude arrived in Memphis, she sought the help of family members. Sadly, no one's financial or living situation was such that they could provide for additional mouths to feed. She found no one who would or could take them in. Therefore, Maude did the only thing she could do—she gave her children away.

It was easier to find homes for the boys. Boys could milk cows, chop wood, and pick cotton; they could earn their keep. Cousins offered to take in the boys, and Maude agreed. What choice did she have? To save them, she had to let them go. The girls proved more difficult to place, but over time other families agreed to take them, all except my grandmother, the baby, the youngest. She was placed in an orphanage.

Maude had no job. Her final task was to find one to support herself. Miraculously, she did, in the same town as the orphanage. I cannot imagine the relief she felt at finding a job and the incredible heartache of giving her children away. My heart longs to know all that she was thinking and feeling as she struggled to survive day by day. Did pain and remorse define her days, or did she thank God for His provision? Did she have faith that God had her and her children in the palm of His hand, or was she angry with Him? Did she believe she had a purpose and a destiny, or was she just defeated? How alone she must have felt. I am sure this was not how she imagined her life would be. This was not her happily ever after.

Meet Eleanor and Benjamin

In another small Tennessee town lived a loving couple. Though they had everything money could buy, the one and only thing their hearts truly desired—children—was denied to them. While they hoped and prayed for little ones to hold, Benjamin Lee Thomas and Eleanor Glass Thomas lived a generous life, helping those in need in their community. They lived by the motto, "But by the grace of God, there go I," and responded immediately to any injustices they saw, especially those involving children. Not only did they respond monetarily to the needs they encountered, but they also loved and served the people with those needs. Though physically barren, they remained pregnant with the possibility of having a child.

Somehow, Benjamin and Eleanor heard about Maude, her situation, and my grandmother in the orphanage. Following their hearts to help, they left their hometown in Milan, Tennessee, and booked a train ride to Memphis to meet Maude. I wonder, did they know it was a journey to their destiny, their long-awaited daughter, my grandmother, and eventually to me, their great-granddaughter? Probably not. They heard of a need, and they responded.

They met Maude and began to build a relationship. They were also introduced to my grandmother at the orphanage during those visits. They made the journey three times during the early months of 1914, continuing to ponder how they may help Maude and her children. By this time, my grandmother was almost two years old, and along the way, Benjamin and Eleanor fell in love with her. They invited Maude to visit their home to see how and where they lived. They continued going to Memphis to visit her, my grandmother, and eventually all of Maude's children. Even though Maude had a job, she could only afford a room to rent in someone else's home.

After many visits and hours sharing their hearts, the Thomases offered to adopt my grandmother. They wanted to give her a new home, a new family, and a new life. They offered what I imagine was a difficult choice for Maude. A new name and a new identity for her daughter. Was it hard or easy for Maude to say yes? Examining my own momma's heart, I am sure it was extremely difficult to say goodbye to her child and offer her to another. How my heart aches for her choice! What unselfish love my great-grandmother Maude demonstrated to her daughter, my grandmother.

The day Benjamin and Eleanor took my grandmother to their home, they adopted her into their hearts. She was their long-awaited daughter. They called her family, giving her their name and a new one of her own, "Elizabeth," which means God's promise. That is who she was to them—a promise fulfilled.

My grandmother loved her adoption story and her new name. She believed it reflected her identity and solidified her destiny. With adoption, her life changed. She was now the beloved daughter of Benjamin and Eleanor Thomas, not an abandoned child left in an orphanage. She had a place where she belonged, and no one could take that away from her. She believed she had the same rights and privileges as a biological child and saw evidence of it daily, as the Thomases loved her as if she had been born from Eleanor's body. Her identity became one of being chosen, redeemed, and loved. Because of that new identity, my grandmother came to believe she could change the world! And the best part of the story, she always knew her biological mother and siblings, as the Thomases encouraged and invited relationships between them all. They weren't trying to take something away; they were trying to give something away.

Love.

Family.

Identity.

Belonging.

We all need those things to be and do all we were created to.

I love this story of my grandmother's, my Mimi's, adoption. It mirrors our own. It does not matter how or as whom we started this life. It matters not what circumstances we have been through—pain, death, infertility, poverty, or even abuse. They are no match for the extravagant love and good plans our Creator, our Heavenly Father, has for us, His adopted children. We are His, and He loves us madly. We cannot change our past, but adoption into God's family can change our identity and destiny.

This journey of identity is one that we should not seek answers from only other human beings. Our love for each other is flawed and imperfect, just like us. Start with your Creator, the One who made you. Ask Him, "Who did You create me to be?" You can trust His affirmations and His still, small voice. Take a long walk and listen for His voice—His confirmation of who you are. Journal your thoughts, questions, and the old identity labels you or someone else has given you. Contemplate what exchanging them for *beloved, adopted,* and *planned* would mean. What would the implications be of embracing and living out of them?

You can experience the freedom that comes from knowing your true identity as a child of God. Your inheritance is a world-changing destiny that will change you and others, birthed out of this identity. You can be secure in this identity and courageously act out of it, even if it takes a while for all the implications to sink in. It certainly did for me.

Facing My Fears

My husband owns his own business; he is a natural gas consultant. We have worked together since the year 2000. At one particular time in our business life, our natural gas supplier informed us that we would have to obtain letters of credit from all of our clients or we would no longer be able to purchase our natural gas. This simple revelation meant we would have no business, thus, no jobs or income without those letters of credit. Let's just say this proclamation produced a tad bit of stress in our home.

Before our supplier's phone call, I had begun living out my new identity as a beloved child of God. I was giddy with the implications of being created on purpose for a purpose. I had even made strides in discovering what this purpose may even be. For the first time in thirty years, I was authentically me and loving every minute of it until my husband declared that obtaining the letters of credit was *my* new job responsibility! I did not even know what a letter of credit was, much less how to get one. My boss (i.e., my husband) offered no advice except, "Figure it out, or we lose the business." (No pressure whatsoever!)

When tasked with this daunting project, I felt like I was ten years old again, standing in the principal's office. *I am about to be embarrassed, humiliated, and ashamed if I attempt this.* It seemed imminent, or so I convinced myself. For days, I did nothing. Fear paralyzed me. Suddenly, I could not access my new identity. Until one day, I received an unexpected but much-needed phone call. It was a dear woman, my spiritual mentor, Terri Fenwick.

"What are you doing?" she asked.

Without taking a breath or uttering any pleasantries, I blurted out my predicament. I was blatantly hoping to receive sympathy from her for the incredible burden and responsibility my husband had saddled me with. She and her husband owned their own business, so I thought she would commiserate with me. Much to my surprise, I got neither from Miss Terri. Instead, she confronted me, "How many phone calls have you made to the bankers?"

"None," I whispered in my most pitiful voice.

"Why?"

"I have no idea what to say, what I need, or what I am asking for," I whined. "I feel like an idiot."

"What are you wearing?" she asked.

What am I wearing? I could not figure out what that had to do with my situation. "Uh, my workout clothes from the gym?"

With a very firm and forceful voice, she told me something I have never forgotten: "Go take a shower right now, then put on your very best clothes and do your make-up and hair. After that, I want you to make ten phone calls to banks this afternoon, expecting with each one that you will receive exactly what you ask for. Jenny, you are the daughter of God, and His favor rests upon you. Act like it."

Then she hung up. This entire situation seemed like a divine test in claiming and acting out of my true identity.

Terri's words empowered my heart and seemed to add steel to my backbone. She was right. I was a child of God! As that realization settled in my mind again, I no longer felt like an embarrassed ten-year-old, frightened child. I was no longer afraid of being humiliated. I was nervous, but I was no longer paralyzed. I did what Terri said. I took a shower, and I took courage. Then I made those calls. With each one made, I gained more and more confidence, even though I received many very polite no's. It didn't matter. I grew bolder with each call, gaining experience and knowledge along the way. This situation allowed me to practice being me—the confident, bold me I was made to be.

I made a choice. I chose to act out of my new identity. *It did not matter what I felt.* I could choose. The old fears and negative feelings no longer held me hostage. My true identity was now securely in place, though I needed a bit of a reminder. I continued to make those calls with complete confidence, expecting great favor. Finally, through a series of truly miraculous events, we received the letters of credit we needed to continue our business, all because I had the courage to be me.

Another lesson I learned through that experience was that both my husband and God could see my true identity easier than I could. At the beginning of my journey of purpose, I was fortunate as they both believed in me more than I did myself. To prove it, both seemed to be throwing me into the deep end so I could learn to walk on water.

We must stop seeking our identity and sense of self-worth from others, the past, what we do, whom we date or are married to, the title before or after our name, or how we perform. If we do, that identity will come crashing down if we get divorced, fired, or fail. Those are all external roles, not an internal awareness of who we are despite external circumstances.

This concept can be difficult for those of us who did not receive the love, blessings, and affirmation from a biological father or mother when we were growing up. I recognize it can be very difficult to have a positive connotation of a Heavenly Father or adopted family if your experience with an earthly one was abusive, distant, or neglectful. It is hard to believe in others, much less yourself, when you have been bestowed a false or negative identity. If this has been your experience, I am so sorry. How I wish I could change that reality and experience for you. I acknowledge that this journey of identity will be more difficult for you and may take more time to truly embrace than those who had a family who believed in and loved them. You may consider visiting a professional counselor or therapist to assist you in this identity journey. I encourage it! You do not lack faith by making this choice. You are showing faith in yourself by making such a choice.

While the past cannot be changed, you can make choices that will shape your future. Old labels and identities can be replaced with new ones that reflect your true self. You are now called *beloved*. You have a place where you *belong*. You are *planned*, *unique*, and *an original*. You have a *destiny*. That is your true identity. Believing it will change everything.

CHAPTER 4

Beloved. Belong. Believe.

Beloved. Belong. Believe.

I love these words. They resound deep within me, providing a much-needed melody to my soul. They soothe and encourage me. I want to be called *beloved* by another. I need a place to *belong*, where I am a part of something bigger than myself. I long to *believe* that the world, or at least someone, needs me to be me. Beloved. Belong. Believe. These words reveal the secret desires of my heart, all of our hearts.

To live from and make choices out of our true identity, we need to hear these and other affirming words to change the often-negative narrative we have playing inside of us. Words like these are essential to changing the tape and are ingredients of water-walking, giant-slaying, history-making destinies. When we know we are *loved* and have a place to *belong*, it becomes much easier to entertain and *believe* that we have a world-changing destiny. Belief allows the impossible to become possible and the ordinary to become extraordinary. Subsequently, behaviors that do not align with our true identity—those keeping us from our destiny—will slowly change, aligning with how we think and feel about ourselves and our potential.

Beloved.

In Henri Nouwen's book *Parting Words*, he talks about the identity of the beloved.

> I very much believe the core moment of Jesus' public life was the baptism in the Jordan, when Jesus heard the affirmation, "You are my beloved on whom my favor rests." That is the core experience of Jesus. He is reminded in a deep, deep way of who he is. The temptations in the desert are temptations to move him away from that spiritual identity. He was tempted to believe he was someone else: You are the one who can turn stone into bread. You are the one who can jump from the temple. You are the one who can make others bow to your power. Jesus said, "No, no, no. I am the Beloved from God." I think his whole life is continually claiming that identity in the midst of everything … Prayer, then, is listening to that voice—to the One who calls YOU beloved. It is to constantly go back to the truth of who we are and claim it for ourselves. I'm not what I do, I'm not what people say about me. I'm not what I have. Although there is nothing wrong with success, there is nothing wrong with popularity, there is nothing wrong with being powerful, but my spiritual identity is not rooted in the world, the things the world gives me. My life is rooted in my spiritual identity. Whatever we do, we have to go back regularly to that place of core identity—you are mine; you are beloved.[1]

Being called *beloved* is the first step of identity boot camp. Knowing we are loved is essential to believe we matter. Others may or may not have called you beloved. Human love is fickle at best and very often dependent upon our behavior, performance, or ability to meet the needs of another. Loving ourselves, even liking ourselves, becomes our own responsibility and is paramount to the journey. To get to this place of loving yourself, you must carefully assess who you are and who you are not. It is very interesting how others will love you to the degree that you love yourself. That is why consulting your Creator is so important to this process. He made you. He delights in you. He can explain you to you— the why of you and what He was thinking when He knit you together in your mother's womb.

God unveils His intentions for you through the lens of His extravagant love. He sees who you are supposed to be, who He created you to be. He does not see what you lack. He sees your potential and uses His love to transform you into a water-walking, giant-slaying, history-making individual. It will absolutely take courage to be and do all you were created to, but it will also require that you choose to see yourself as God sees you and hear Him whisper *beloved*.

You now have a choice. You can choose to embrace this identity of beloved or not. If you do embrace it, it may be the most courageous decision you ever make. It is very difficult to love someone who does not love themselves. It is also tough to embark on an exciting journey of purpose without loving yourself. Loving yourself may take practice if the concept is new to you. Having a place to belong helps.

Belong.

People have an insatiable desire to belong to something bigger than themselves. As soon as we are weaned from our mother's breast or the bottle, the desire to attach our independent selves to another person or group begins. Both little girls and boys alike seem to announce their pick of a best friend as soon as they launch into their first social situation. Playdates and birthday parties ensue.

Today's definition of "good parenting" demands that a child join as many organized groups as possible as early as possible. Girl Scouts and Boy Scouts, dance troupes, choirs, martial arts, drama, and every sport imaginable all offer a child a place to belong. As we get older, neither the desire nor the groups diminish. Book clubs, supper clubs, bars, and country clubs are on the menu to meet this need in us as adults. We are so desperate to belong that we are even willing to pay money for the privilege of adding our names to a group's exclusive roster. We long to belong—to attach our names to one another.

We should not be surprised by our strong need to belong and our aversion to being alone. We started life literally attached to our mother. We were then birthed into a group, a family.

I am Jenny, the oldest daughter of four children, a single entity. However, I *belong* to a family that numbers hundreds of aunts, uncles, cousins, and grandparents. When we are all together, I truly feel a part of something bigger than myself. Being a part of a family gives me a shared name and identity. Though now married, I was born a *Thornton*. That one word meant we were resilient, independent, confident, loud, athletic, and hardworking. We even had a family motto, a collective identity: *We bend, but we do not break*. I can see glimpses of myself in the generations before and after me. It feels good to be connected to this group. When we are together, the longing to belong is appeased, at least for a time. However, being in one place simultaneously is very difficult and rarely happens because we are all scattered across the United States.

The movies we love often highlight this longing to belong. Do you remember the classic line from the 1996 movie *Jerry Maguire*? (I am so dating myself!) Tom Cruise's character whispers to Renee Zellweger's character, "You complete me."[2] Every woman who heard those words at the movie theater gasped as her secret desire was broadcast on the screen so simply and clearly from an actor's lips straight to our own hearts. Romantic love, belonging to another, is something we all believe will complete us. However, in the long run, we discover that no one person can complete us.

While marriage was designed to give us that sense of belonging, to be a place where two separate, unique individuals come together to become one, many relationships and marriages fail. When that happens, that sense of oneness and belonging becomes a pain-filled process, leaving both parties profoundly alone and disconnected. In my life, I have experienced both—the pain of divorce and an incredible marriage going on thirty-one years. I love that sense of belonging in a marriage, but I also know how fragile it can be.

Friendship is another profound way I have experienced unity that creates a sense of belonging. Many have said that friends are the family you get to choose. I agree. There are people in my life on whom I have bestowed the identity of *my friend*, but that title cannot describe what they mean to my heart. One of the kids in our clan coined the phrase *God-family* to describe friends who become family. Time and distance cannot diminish the bond and the oneness we share. These friendships are divine, and they are also created *on purpose for a purpose*. We belong to each other. We regularly share our hearts and holidays, burdens and bread, joys and sorrows. We generously serve, love, and give to each other. We share every aspect of our lives. These relationships help me feel like I am not all alone in this world. These people encourage me to be and do all I was created to. They believe in me. I belong . . . until one of us moves away, gets divorced, or the relationship becomes broken. Then I feel alone again.

When healthy, all of these attachments and relationships *can* provide us with a much-needed sense of belonging and an identity that intertwines with others—temporarily. It does not matter how many groups we belong to or identify with; each of us will find ourselves, at one time or another, alone or lonely, divorced or estranged, left or abandoned. This is incredibly painful and can breed a host of emotions lethal to discovering or holding on to your newly discovered identity.

That is why we must consult our Creator. He promised never to leave us alone or abandon us. He adopted us into His family, providing an irrevocable place for us to belong. This place is not based on effort or performance. He loved us first. He chooses us and offers a mysterious completeness that other human beings and groups can never provide. I learned this the hard way, and you will probably have to as well. People will never complete me. Your relationships will never complete you. People, and our relationships with them, are imperfect, just as we are.

When we grasp this truth, it takes the pressure off our relationships, and we can just enjoy them. We stop the frantic search to belong, putting pressure on others to meet these deep emotional needs for belonging.

A bride and groom. Families. Friendships. All these relationships were to be a glimpse, an imperfect copy of the original design God intended for us to experience in our relationship with Him. He wants to give you a permanent place to belong so you are no longer sifting through the rubble of earthly relationships looking to a mere human being to provide only what He can. As I learned this lesson, my relationships with people became stronger because I no longer depended on them to validate me. I knew I had a place where I belonged. Now I know that I am never alone. I know my identity and that I have a world-changing destiny. Do you?

I encourage you to look to your Creator to solidify this truth within you. You are called *beloved*. You have a place to *belong*. The next step is choosing to *believe*.

Believe.

Did you know what you believe can have nothing to do with *truth?*

I remember helping my boys with their fourth-grade world history homework years ago. We laughed at the "truths" that most people believed during the Middle Ages about our earth. What they then called truth we now call silly—even to fourth-grade boys.

1. The world was flat, and if you tried to sail to the edge, you would fall off the edge.
2. If you sailed near the equator, your skin would turn black.
3. A great sea monster would eat you alive if you sailed a certain distance from home.

We all laugh at those truths now. They seem ridiculous. However, long ago, many people believed and based their choices on these commonly held truths, even though they were completely false. Their beliefs produced an emotion, fear, which caused them to choose to stay very close to home. Their false beliefs produced self-limiting behaviors that kept them from exploring the world and their destiny. That is until a man came along and courageously and publicly challenged the widely held "truth" of the day. He changed the world by embarking on a journey to prove what they believed was not true.

We can do exactly the same thing for ourselves. We need to examine, evaluate, and challenge the truths we hold about ourselves.

Truth. Your truth. My truth. The truth. Is there a difference? Absolutely. However, in our society, these words are often used interchangeably. Declaring something as "my truth" can create false and counterproductive impressions that truth is fluid and not a consistent and unavoidable reality with which we must contend.

Merriam-Webster's dictionary defines *truth* as "the real facts about something: the things that are true."[3] It is not derived from our experiences or perceptions, or beliefs.

Today, we are all being encouraged to own and share "our truth," which can and is often different from "the truth." The encouragement is correct, but the word is wrong. "In my experience" or "from my perspective" lends itself to a better descriptor. You and I can have a shared experience and completely different takeaways about that experience. Therefore, by today's definition, we could have different truths about the same situation when what we really have is another point of view or perspective.

We are all positioned differently in life, with different experiences, family histories, socioeconomic status, personalities, and physiological make-ups. Some of us are raised in the same family, have the same experiences, and come away with entirely different takeaways based on our personalities, birth order, or lived experiences, whether negative or positive. Some of us have experienced traumas that bestow lies upon us about who we are and the world around us.

In my work with trafficking victims, I have heard over and over again the belief that there are no good men in this world. Is that true? No. However, it is very easy to understand why they hold this as truth from their perspective—it is their experience. A lie that traffickers exploit for many victims is that the people who love you physically hurt you. Again, this becomes their truth because of their experience. Many victims I have worked with believe that "no one cares" and that they "have no value." Traffickers, who can even be family members, exploit this belief and provide repeated experiences confirming that no one cares and they have no value. Since this is their lived experience, it sadly becomes their truth, one they eventually agree with, then live and act out of. That is, unless or until someone comes along and provides them with new evidence and a new truth about their worth and value. This has been one of the greatest joys of my life, watching this happen firsthand.

While I have not experienced any trauma that would come close to what these young ones have endured, I did believe and act out of a lie that I held as truth for over thirty years because of an experience. Remember when my ten-year-old self was subjected to the principal's ridicule of my dreams and values? For the first time in my young life, I *felt* embarrassed and humiliated. At that moment, I assumed that *I* was the embarrassment. Something was wrong with *me*, so at the ripe old age of ten, I vowed to stop being me. The thoughts made me *feel* strong negative emotions that produced a narrative I agreed with. It became my truth, one that I acted out of for many years, even though it was a lie.

Did you catch that? My thoughts produced my emotions, ultimately influencing my choices and behaviors for many years. All this happened with lightning speed in my brain.

Unconsciously, because I was too young and inexperienced to do anything different, I began a systematic reprogramming of myself. I didn't have the strength of self to share the experience with anyone so they could pour truth over the lie. I buried the experience in my little girl's heart where it went unexamined for over thirty years but had the power to produce self-limiting behaviors. Those behaviors betrayed the belief I had about myself. I had predictable, defaulted behaviors ready to erupt during any potentially embarrassing situation. Don't stand out! Don't raise your hand! Be silent! Dress alike, talk alike, hide in plain sight . . . assimilate! I created comfort zones that ensured against the possibility of embarrassment. I never tried anything new or anything I was not naturally good at. Little did I know that these comfort zones, the ones I thought protected me, were actually the enemy of my soul. The lies that I had embraced as truth and the subsequent coping behaviors robbed me of my destiny for years. If left unexamined, lies can do that to yours too.

"The truth may be out there, but the lies are inside your head."

—Terry Pratchett

CHAPTER 5

Examine What Is True

"Discovering the truth about ourselves is a lifetime's
work, but it is worth the effort."

—*Fred Rogers*

It is possible for what we believe to have nothing to do with truth. Our beliefs, behaviors, choices, and, subsequently, our actions could all be based upon a lie or multiple lies we have internalized as truth—our truth. So where do we find the actual truth about ourselves?

Psychologists call our erroneous beliefs *negative core narratives.* These lies are often established early in childhood due to negative and/or traumatic experiences. Our positive beliefs and core narratives do not pose many problems for us. But the negative or false ones can distort the truth, limit our behaviors, and entice us to settle for much less than we were created for. If left unexamined, they become our engrained truth and provide the lens for how we view others, our Creator, the world, and ourselves. They become the unconscious programming in our brain from where our behavior originates—default behaviors. Let's break it down with this diagram:

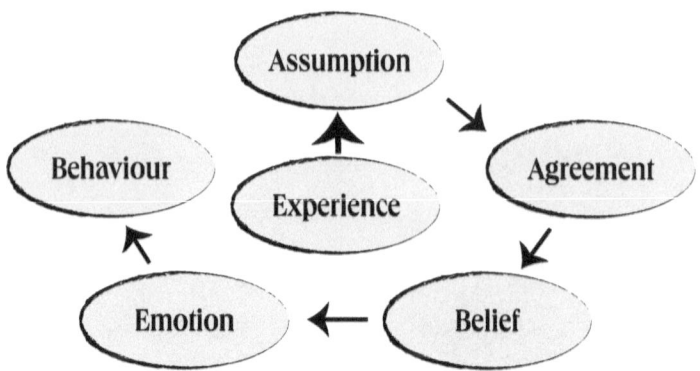

At the center is an experience. That experience produces an assumption, a thought which tells us whether the experience is good or bad. In the blink of an eye, we come in agreement about the experience, and that agreement then produces a belief which then produces an emotion—positive if good, negative if bad. If good, we want to replicate that experience. If bad, we want to avoid it at all costs. The brain is such an amazing organ!

What we think and how we feel about an experience will produce a behavior aligning with those beliefs and feelings. It becomes "our truth" and a defaulted behavior you give no thought to unless examined. That belief produces an emotion that constructs our behaviors. We do not even have to think about them. Our brains just keep speeding up the process until those behaviors become defaulted, predictable knee-jerk reactions that occur when we sense the emotion or potential of the unwanted emotion.

Think of it this way. A newly purchased computer has an internal software program. It has two operating modes: default and design. The default mode creates actions that automatically happen in certain situations without the operator issuing a specific command. It is easy because it has been programmed.

The design mode is much more complicated. To invoke all the software's complex applications, the extensive operating manual or the actual creator of the program must be consulted for the computer to do all it was created to do.

Do you consult the manual when you buy a new computer to optimize performance? Not me. I like quick, easy, and automatic. Unfortunately, I lived that way for many years, and my default behaviors kept me from all I was designed for. Yours may be, too.

We are not much different from a computer. We, too, have default and design modes. We are highly complex with great potential, but at the same time, we can operate on autopilot, doing less than we were designed for. We are able to proceed throughout our day, acting and reacting to stimuli and situations without much thought. We do this because our default mode is much simpler than our design mode. Our culture, our family, and our experiences have programmed us. We have become comfortable with our familiar, predictable, and automatic behaviors, even if we do not necessarily like them.

We act as if we have no control over them. But that is not true. That is a lie. We can literally take every thought captive before it becomes a freight train wreaking havoc in our lives. Our default mode is what keeps us from our destiny. It is crazy to keep doing the same things over and over again expecting a different outcome. Yet we do.

Again, positive reactions and behaviors are not the problem. The negative core beliefs or narratives will keep us from being and doing all we were created to. We must get off autopilot. We must examine our programming. We must dig deep. We all have behaviors we want to change. When we muster up the courage to try to change those behaviors, we fail because we have not challenged the belief that produces the emotions that helped construct the default behavior. We get frustrated and quit because we do not see the results we long for. We come in agreement with the lie that we are failures. We hate the emotions that belief produces, so we vow to live with our unwanted, self-limiting behaviors. Around and around, we go on this merry-go-round of defeat, never being and doing what we were created to do.

As humans, we focus and spend so much time and money trying to change our behaviors. We try to lose weight, quit smoking, stop drinking, and more, but so many of our behaviors are typical symptoms of deep-rooted emotions that spring from false beliefs or lies implanted in us, typically during our childhood. I found that when I began to examine my negative, unwanted behaviors, I could trace them all back to a lie or a label that someone bestowed upon me or a lie I had bestowed upon myself. However, I discovered that if I wanted to change a behavior, I first had to identify the feelings and negative beliefs associated with it. Then the behavior became easy to change by replacing the lie with the truth.

Consult Your Creator

To find the truth about ourselves, we must ask why. We must be authentically self-aware. We must be mindful of the stored experiences and the beliefs they produce that may not be true. The *why* of the belief is the key to change. It is the bull's-eye we must hit. My behaviors and emotions were easy to identify but cloaked the belief. To determine whether my beliefs were true or not, I had to consult my Creator. I decided I was tired of living out of my default mode;

I wanted to operate from design. It was a rigorous process that yielded great results in my life that can be replicated in yours.

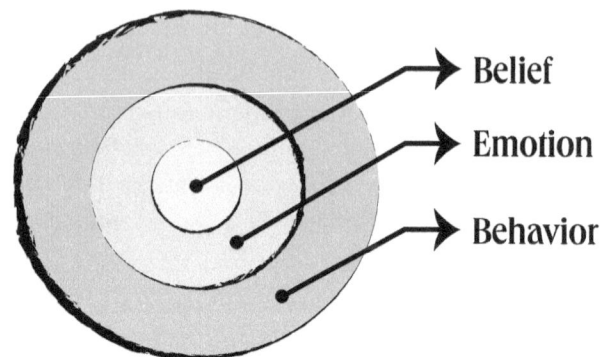

I started with the obvious—my unwanted default behaviors. I examined my avoidance of anything that had the potential to produce feelings of embarrassment or humiliation, which can be just about anything except breathing. What are negative default behaviors that may be keeping you from being you? Write them down. To identify them, pay close attention to your intense emotional reactions to seemingly benign situations, situations where you react or overreact without cause. Anger, rage, sweaty palms, a racing heart, and abject fear are all clues to situations that do not warrant those reactions. Do not gloss over the behavior with rationalizations; instead, begin to ask *why* of your Maker. Examine these negative narratives to determine if they are clouding your identity and limiting your destiny.

If you had asked me ten years ago to go on a stage, make a presentation, or speak to a group of more than four people, all of which I now frequently do, I would have run screaming for the hills. I would become physically ill at just the thought of public speaking. Even to me, that response seemed an overreaction. Why? I did not know. I never once questioned it; I just avoided it like the plague until I had the courage to examine it.

When I began this journey of uncovering my identity and discovering my destiny, I realized I had avoided many things that I once loved as a child. Things like athletic competitions, having an opinion, speaking up, and being on stage. Deep in my brain, I believed it would be embarrassing to lose, have a different opinion, or, God forbid, have everyone look at me and freeze with nothing to say. Irrationally, I argued with anyone about anything because I believed it was embarrassing to be wrong. These scenes were too risky for one as frightened of embarrassment as me, so I avoided them or went into attack mode. All of these behaviors were my default mode; they required no thought on my part but happened automatically if I sensed potential embarrassment or humiliation. They stemmed from the erroneous belief that I was an embarrassment. I constantly felt unsettled in my soul because any activity or conversation had the potential for the feared feelings. My behavior betrayed my belief about myself.

What would happen if you examined your negative beliefs? Can you change them? Can you apply truth and stop them from limiting your behaviors and robbing you of your destiny? Would your life really change? Yes! Yes! Yes!

A core narrative always begins with *I am*—negative or positive. We will focus on the negative here, with a few examples to get you thinking about the negative tapes running in your head.

I am an embarrassment.	*I am ugly.*
I am unplanned.	*I am an accident.*
I am of no value.	*I am unlovable.*
I am unattractive.	*I am insignificant.*
I am unworthy.	*I am the problem.*
I am unintelligent.	

Do you see how any of these statements could bestow a false identity upon us *if* we agree with them? When we come in agreement with them, they become a belief. These negative and untrue beliefs produce strong emotions and feelings we begin to act out of. Your behaviors will always betray your beliefs. Let me explain it this way.

If you believe you are unlovable, you will feel unlovable and eventually act unlovable. If you think you are unintelligent, you feel stupid and will act that way. You will feel ugly and display ugly behaviors if you believe you are ugly. If you believe you have no value, you will feel insignificant and invisible and make choices that reflect that belief and those feelings. All those behaviors, after a while, become second nature to you. They become your default mode.

Are light bulbs going off? Any flashes of lightning? Is the haze clearing?

Your behaviors stem from who you *believe* you are. What is extremely frightening is that these beliefs may or may not be true!

When God challenged me with the question, "Do you have the courage to be you . . . the you I created?" it caused me to ask *Who am I?* and *Who did you create me to be?* I started to examine why I would overreact to seemingly insignificant slights and certain situations. I questioned why I stopped doing things I once loved and became silent. That question caused me to feel like I was settling for less than I was created for and ultimately caused me to willingly take the time necessary to examine my negative core narratives and expose them to the truth. I knew I could not trust myself or another person for the truth, so I consulted my Creator.

Where were the lies? When did they start? What is true about me? I asked the questions and journeyed through the process. It was truly life-changing. I remembered the false identities and negative labels bestowed upon me by others and myself. *Too* loud, *too* bossy, *too* embarrassing; the message I received and the lie I believed was clear—I was *too much*. During this process, I began to see how I had intentionally dumbed myself down and limited my potential with my negative beliefs.

You are too much and *You are not enough* seem to be two common negative core narratives that greatly limit people's behavior. Neither is true! We must stop this merry-go-round of negative thoughts, beliefs, feelings, and behaviors if we are going to be and do all we were created to be and do!

First, examine your defaulted, unwanted behaviors, the ones that make no sense but are repetitive. They are usually pretty obvious. Next, identify the emotions associated with that behavior. Do not ignore or run from them. Your feelings are the link between your behavior and belief, which may or may not be true. My goal is to expose the lie, not make you feel bad.

Here are some examples to get you thinking:

Unwanted Behavior	Emotion Produced
I always **walk out** when I feel angry.	**Anger** produced the unwanted behavior.
I always **quit** if I feel embarrassed.	The feeling of **embarrassment** caused the quitting.
I always **lie** if I feel worried.	Feeling **worried** preempted the lying.
I **steal** when I feel inadequate or do not measure up to others.	Feeling **inadequate** rationalized the criminal behavior.
I **cheat** on tests when I feel stupid.	Feeling **stupid** caused the unethical behavior.
I **sleep around** when I feel undesirable.	Feeling **ugly** produced an unhealthy choice.
I always **eat too much** when I feel sad.	Feeling **sad** caused the overeating.
I always **drink excessively** when I feel stressed financially.	**Stress** produces the excess.

Now see if you can determine the belief that caused the emotion that produced the behavior. Remember, we are focusing on the negative and unwanted ones. Pay attention to statements that begin with always, no one, and never. Sentences containing those words can provide clues to negative programming. Again, behaviors and emotions are much easier to ascertain than hidden beliefs. At this point in the process, it is imperative that you consult your Creator.

Erroneous Beliefs · · · Negative Feelings · · · Subsequent Behaviors

- I believe I will always hit someone if I get angry;
  - I feel afraid,
    - so I walk out during any confrontation or argument.

- I believe I will always be laughed at if I try something new;
  - I feel embarrassed,
    - so I quit, or worse, I never try.

- I believe I will always hurt someone's feelings if I speak the truth;
  - I fear rejection,
    - so I flatter them or lie to them.

- I believe no one will like me for myself;
  - I feel inadequate,
    - so I steal things to make myself seem cooler.

- I believe I will never go to college;
  - I feel dumb,
    - so I cheat on all my tests.

- I believe I am not attractive and will never marry;
  - I feel undesirable,
    - so I sleep with anyone who shows interest in me.

- I believe I will never be happy;
  - I feel sad,
    - so I eat to try and make the feeling go away.

- I believe I will never have enough money to pay my bills;
  - I feel overwhelmed,
    - so I drink to forget.

Do you see how any one of these erroneous beliefs can produce negative feelings and subsequent behaviors that could keep someone from being and doing all they were created to? It is much easier to see the connections when we write them down. Please do not worry if you cannot make all the connections right now. Some of my own discoveries and connections took a great deal of time to uncover.

As I promised you at the beginning of our journey, I am trying to put tangible steps together to expedite your timeline of uncovering your true identity and fulfilling your destiny. However, your Creator provides the ultimate connections and timing. For now, it's okay to have some gaps and blanks. Trust the One who made you. He will provide all your answers at just the right time.

There is one last step in this process. You need to see if you can remember what incident or experience produced your inaccurate belief or beliefs. When I was younger, I had multiple negative experiences and disappointments. We all do. However, I discovered there was really only one where I had made a vow that caused me to stop being myself: the incident at the principal's office. You may also have had just one incident, or you may have had multiple ones. We are each unique, and there is no exact formula that applies to us universally. Consult your Creator for any experience(s) where you made a vow that has had the greatest impact on your identity and could right now be robbing you of your destiny.

You can recognize the core narratives and lies because they always start with *I am*. The vow or subsequent assumption that comes afterward always begins with the word *so*.

My story may seem mild compared to what you have experienced or suffered. However, it greatly impacted my life for many years. Digging for answers through our memories may require a professional therapist, counselor, or life coach if your experiences are severe or traumatic. I encourage you to take that step. Consulting your Creator through this process is also a must, and a professional may be the vehicle He uses to guide you on this journey. Be open to the process. Ask the questions. Start with examining any of your behaviors or habits that you would like to change and see if you can determine the incident that produced a false belief and negative emotion. Determine if you made a vow that you believed would protect you but hindered you from being you instead.

The Truth Changes Everything

Your beliefs may have nothing to do with truth, but you can change what you believe—with truth.

Your Creator has all of your answers. He knows your design mode because He created it. As with our computer analogy, you are much more complex, created for more than your default, destiny-limiting behaviors. He knows who He created you to be.

When I consulted my Creator and specifically asked God, *"Who am I, and who did you create me to be?"* I did not hear my own familiar negative core narratives: "You are an embarrassment, you are too bossy, too loud, too much." Instead, these words of affirmation were whispered into my heart, "You are vivacious, you are a good communicator, you are a strong leader, you are mine." Daily, as I continued to consult my Creator within the pages of my journal, new words and new beliefs about myself were downloaded to my spirit until I had a new vocabulary describing me! Every negative thought and subsequent lie I believed about me was exposed, examined, and then replaced with truth by the One who made me. These were words I wanted to believe about me and for me. These words were the ones I now came in agreement with. It took much discipline. I wrote them down on five-by-seven cards and read them out loud every single day three times a day for months before they silenced the lies I had believed for years.

I am a good communicator.

I am a strong leader.

I am not an embarrassment.

I am victorious.

I am vivacious. (I love that word!)

I am a child of God, created on purpose for a purpose.

I have a destiny.

I am beloved.

I belong.

I was planned.

This was my new identity. My job now was simply to believe. In the beginning, believing was a daily choice, not a feeling. As I practiced my new truth aloud, my thoughts began to change, and miraculously so did my feelings! When that happened, the self-limiting, unwanted behaviors started to align with the truth I chose to believe about myself. When the written words became my truth, I began to act and operate out of my design mode confidently. It felt unnatural at first. It even took a great deal of courage for me to leave the known for the unknown. However, when I did, I discovered that many activities that once scared me to death were the very ones God designed as a part of my identity and destiny. Though I took baby steps at first, even the people in my life began to notice the changes in me as I made strides toward my destiny. I even started speaking on a stage and loved it!

This journey requires faith in what you do not see. Many people use the words *faith* and *belief* interchangeably, but *faith is belief that is not based on proof.*[4]

Sounds rather unintelligent, doesn't it? The Bible has a definition I like much better:

*Faith is being sure of what we hope for
and certain of what we cannot see.*

Hebrews 11:1 NIV

Having confidence in what we *cannot* see at this moment but what we believe will be—that is having faith in yourself. That is what your identity boot camp is for—to convince you that you are who God says you are and that you have what it takes to do what He created you to do.

Negative or positive repetition has the same outcome—either one will become a well-worn path in our brain that will produce emotions that will affect our behaviors. It can be a negative rut we are stuck in or a positive path to our purpose. You can reverse the process of negativity with this truth:

*Before time began, you were created on purpose for a
purpose. You have a great destiny awaiting you.*

Examine what you believe and why you believe it. Change your truth. You do have the courage to be you! Repeat these words with me until you have the faith to believe:

I am beloved. I do belong. I have a destiny. I will believe.

Get your truth cards out and daily repeat the words you have written. I give you permission to be you—the you God created. Sow this truth into your heart:

I am unique, an original work of art. I am fearfully and wonderfully made.

*Before time began, I was known, planned, and loved.
I am no accident. I am meant to be.*

I have a purpose and a destiny.

Now that is the truth!

CHAPTER 6

You Were Planned

When I was twelve, I uncovered a family secret about myself. One weekend, while at my grandmother's house, I was thumbing through the family Bible with my cousin, Tracy. It contained all our family members' recorded births, deaths, and marriages for generations. It was fun reading all the names and looking at the dates. Toward the very end, my birth date was listed, as was the date of my parents' marriage. However, the year was wrong—or so I thought.

I immediately showed the error to my grandmother, the logical choice since she was the matriarch of our family and the only one allowed in this generation to record data in the family Bible. She reviewed the data and promptly guaranteed me that the date of my parents' marriage was correct. No argument. This was recorded truth written in her own handwriting.

But something was very wrong. The math could not be correct. I counted the months again. May, June, July, August, September, October, November. Seven months—not nine—between my parents' wedding date and my birth. The realization slowly began to sink deep within me. My parents had to get married because of me!

I was unplanned.

I did not tell my parents I had learned their secret. Being the child I was, I did not want to embarrass them, especially my mom. I instinctively knew that talking to her about this new truth would do just that.

The news did not rock my twelve-year-old world because I was an extremely well-loved child. I felt wanted my entire life. Discovering my parents' secret did not alter or undermine that truth. It was secure in my heart and a positive core narrative of mine. My parents may not have planned my birth, but they loved me extravagantly throughout my life. Therefore, I buried the secret at the ripe old age of twelve. (Well, I may have let it leak to my siblings.)

While going through my identity boot camp, searching for my identity and destiny, I was talking to my seventy-five-year-old aunt Dean, my mom's oldest sister, on the phone. I knew she had been at the hospital the day I was born. She loved me madly since she had first learned of my existence, planned or not. I shared with her the secret I had kept most of my life. Without hesitation, she proclaimed the truth that traveled two thousand miles through the phone line, straight to my heart. "Oh, darlin', you were no accident. Your life is proof that you were planned by God—on purpose for a purpose."

Warm waves of love flowed over me, on me, and through me. I caught my breath, her words entering the core of who I was. I knew she was right, but I was surprised at how badly I needed to hear them. I did not wrestle with this truth or need to examine it further. I just received it, agreed with it, and believed it. Despite the details of my conception, I knew deep within me that my life was planned on purpose for a purpose, just as my aunt said.

Planned on Purpose

Has anyone ever said these words to you? *You were planned. You are not an accident.*

They are words it seems we all need to hear. I know I did. This positive core narrative is one we all need to embrace and believe.

It does not matter the circumstances surrounding your birth; you were intentionally planned with a specific purpose designed just for you. Since the beginning of time, you have been tenderly thought of and intimately loved by your Creator. That is no accident.

What is your first response when you hear these words? Is it easy for you to believe them? If, like me, you had loving parents, then yes, it is probably easy for you to accept and embrace this truth about yourself. However, if your parents abandoned or abused you or never showed you tangible proof of their love, these words may cause a terrible ache. If that is the case for you, I am so sorry. It is not my intent to cause you any pain. Finding your true identity may take incredible courage on your part. You may need a large dose of courage to believe a loving Creator planned you.

If it is difficult for you to be and do all you were created to and you cannot accept and believe the truth you were planned, consult your Creator. Ask Him to lead you to the evidence of His love. He says that even though your mother and father have forsaken you, He has not and will not. Before time began, you were planned. You are necessary to this world. You are as unique as a work of art. You have been designed to be and do something that no one else on this planet can be or do. Look for the evidence. Look to the actual day of your birth. Are there clues there? Mine had some.

I woke up early on the morning of November 7, 2003. It was my forty-third birthday *and* my eleventh wedding anniversary. (Yes, I got married on my birthday!) The day began like any other: a cup of coffee and a prayer for guidance, provision, and protection. The normal rhythm of an ordinary day—or so I thought. A friend of mine called me to say happy birthday, but she added mysteriously, "God has a special surprise for you today." That was intriguing! No one had ever said anything like that to me before. I was in the third year of my purpose journey, finally realizing my true identity. Daily I was filled with child-like expectancy. Maybe my destiny was just around the corner.

I woke up early that morning to savor the sweet silence of my sleeping children and to open my birthday cards and presents alone. It was a luxury to sip my coffee and read the words lavished on me by my family members and friends without little boys running around. I had almost an hour to myself before I heard the stirring of my precious boys. One last card. Hurriedly, I tore it open, hoping to read it before the boys made it downstairs screaming, "I'm hungry!" The words on the card went straight to my spirit.

> *"On your birthday, I wish for you one perfect*
> *moment when you are utterly yourself,*
>
> *when you are convinced, you are God's own child...*
> *when you realize that everything is within your grasp."*
>
> *—Maya Angelou*

I felt Maya had written those words just for me! I was filled with expectancy. How I wanted to ponder them for hours, but I did not have the time. The boys were dragging their daddy half-awake down the stairs, intent on bestowing homemade cards, birthday wishes, and many kisses on me.

As I cooked breakfast for my boys and my husband (yes, moms cook on their birthday), my mind was visualizing and planning the day: lunch with my girlfriends, phone calls from faraway family, grocery store, takeout for the kids, and then a romantic evening of dancing with my husband for our wedding anniversary. I love to dance.

With the kids off to school and a slew of errands completed, I had a few minutes to shower and get dressed before meeting my friends for lunch. I grabbed the mail before running out the door, just in case more birthday cards arrived.

Among the pile of bills and catalogs, I recognized the handwriting on an envelope buried at the bottom of the pile. It was from one of my favorite people in the world, Aunt Dean, who was there on the day I arrived and reminded me that I was no accident. She had never once missed sending me a card on my birthday. Her cards were always accompanied by a long newsy letter about our family. I assumed today was the same. I anxiously opened her card. Strange. Instead of the long letter, I pulled out a short note in her handwriting.

"I remember the day you were born like it was yesterday. It was such a special day. November 7th. You and Granny share the same birthday."

What? Granny and I were born on the same day? How was this news kept from me for forty-three years? The woman who was not related to me by blood, who had rescued my Mimi from the orphanage and called her daughter, who adopted her into her family, was also born on November 7. I had no idea. Instantly my heart recognized the significance of this news. Time felt like it stopped. It was *evidence* that I was planned. Even the day of my birth was no accident and had great significance. What an amazing birthday gift! I felt like I had just won the lottery. My soul was saturated with love. I burst into tears with this new knowledge. I felt unique, special, and significant. Though I was going to be late for my birthday lunch, I was determined to savor this moment.

I glanced down and touched the thin gold wedding band I wore on my ring finger. It was Granny's wedding ring. My Mimi had given me the ring when I was a teenager. She told me it had belonged to Eleanor, her adoptive mom. She told me how much Granny loved me and that she was at the hospital on the day I was born. (I guess she neglected to tell me we shared the same birthday.)

When I first put the ring on my finger, I marveled that it fit me perfectly. I treasured having this tangible reminder of the woman who rescued my Mimi from an orphanage. It had stayed hidden carefully in a jewelry box until my handsome husband placed it on my finger on our wedding day, November 7, the day Eleanor and I were born. As I touched our ring, I marveled that she was there on the day

I was born, welcoming me, her great-granddaughter by adoption, an unplanned child, into the world on the day of her own birth. It all felt so significant.

At that moment, I believed—no, I *knew*—that our birthdays and destinies were designed to intertwine before time began. I knew it was a sign from my Creator, evidence that my life was planned. I wondered what this woman whispered to me, what prayers she prayed over me at my birth. Did she pass something sacred from her heart to mine in those first moments of my life? I gazed at an old black-and-white photo of us on my desk. She is holding me in her lap. I am a year old. Mimi is standing with us. I am laughing. Three generations created by choice, by adoption not by blood, all planned before time began.

I savor even now how incredibly special I feel just because of the day of my birth. Chosen. Planned. Loved. Set apart. Unique. I was destined for something special, something that only I could do. It all began generations before I was even born. My Creator must have known I would need this additional dose of identity bestowed upon me before I was launched into my destiny. My friend was correct. I had been given an extraordinary gift on my birthday—the knowledge and proof that not only was I planned, but even the day of my birth was significant. It felt like a kiss from heaven.

As I began to believe that I was born at this time in this place for a particular reason, I saw how my parents, grandparents, and great-grandparents were responsible for giving me a firm foundation to stand on. I saw how the ceiling of their life was my floor. I had received a rich heritage from the generations before me—generations of strong, water-walking, giant-slaying men and women who, with faith, believed their Creator for their truth, who took courage to be and do all they were created to. Their past had something to do with my future. I could not wait to find more evidence. I was being wooed into my destiny.

God has surprises planned for you too. Surprises that will confirm your uniqueness and bestow your identity in such a personal way that leaves you feeling special, known, and loved. Your heart is being prepared to receive the details of your destiny. Like Maya Angelou, I wish for you one perfect moment when you are utterly yourself, when you are convinced you are a child of God and everything is within your grasp.

Expect tangible, surprising evidence along your journey to help convince you. Look for proof until you find it. Some clues to your identity and destiny are revealed as surprises when you need them, but others you must look for.

Our Names Matter

Have you considered your name for clues? Do you know its meaning? Names often offer important clues to our identity and destiny. Humans have been bestowing names to give significance since the beginning of recorded history. In distant eras, names bestowed upon children often reflected their parents' feelings or the circumstances during or around their birth. Those feelings or circumstances could be good and bad. At first glance, some names people are saddled with at birth could be a burden or just plain unkind. We need to dig to find our answers.

If you have ever had children, you know the weighty responsibility of bestowing a name upon another human being, a name they will carry throughout their lives. It is a source of great conversations, and even controversy, during the nine months of pregnancy. Almost immediately, the masses of family members ask, "What will you name the baby?" Everyone has an opinion, but no one gets a vote except the parents. Names, just like identities, are bestowed upon us and can provide clues to "who we are."

We Southerners are especially fond of family names. We use our father's names as first names, create double names from our grandfather's names, and frequently use our mother's or even grandmother's maiden names in the mix. Just ask my sons.

Some of us are named after books our parents loved or from the movies they watched. My dad named me Jenny after a movie he saw and loved while my mom was pregnant with me called *The Portrait of Jenny*. While I have never seen the movie, I always loved hearing how I got my name. It was a part of my unique story. My aunt Dean thought Jenny sounded more like a nickname and bestowed the name Jennifer upon me and my birth certificate. No one has ever called me Jennifer. That name never fit me. It sounded too girly and formal for me since I was a tomboy.

When I first discovered the meaning of Jennifer, it confirmed my suspicions that I was not one. Jennifer means *fair one* or *white beauty*. I was neither fair, as in *fair maiden*, nor have I ever felt particularly beautiful. I was a Jenny. However, I hated the definitions I found. Either Jenny was a *donkey* or *a washing machine*, a spinning jenny. My middle name is Lee, inserted by my mom. It was the middle name of my great-grandfather Benjamin. It gave my mom and me the same initials. J. L. T. Jenny Lee. Yikes. I have never loved my name; I thought it was ordinary and plain, like me. It is interesting how my name and self-concept became one and the same. I longed to be called Victoria or Alexandra. Those names sounded so daring and exciting to me. Things I believed I was not—until my journey of purpose.

From an identity and destiny perspective, I never contemplated how much weight a name carries until a trip I took back to my home in the San Francisco Bay area after moving to Sacramento. I would be with the women who had served as my righteous girlfriends—women on a similar journey of purpose. I had been their leader, and I missed them. Unbeknownst to me that day, the new group leader had been researching the names of each group member—mine included. When I arrived, these precious women surrounded me with love and bestowed a gift upon me that I will never forget.

Jenny, your name means courageous, grace-filled, and straight-forward. God wants you to know He sees you, that He has called you by name. Your name is the essence of your life's message.

The words were like living water, and liquid peace poured over my soul. I was stunned. Even my name was not random. I found this new truth to be intoxicating, life-changing, and transforming, especially on this day during a particularly difficult time in my life when I was fighting to keep my identity intact and my dreams alive.

Sobbing ensued as these words went straight to my heart. *Courageous*. Me? I had been scared for most of my life, paralyzed by the fear of embarrassment. However, somewhere inside of me, I remembered the active, courageous little girl I once was. In an instant, the past and present collided in my mind, confirming who I was created to be. Hearing that description of my name that day was like a voice cheering me on, telling me not to quit because I was created to be courageous! Even my name was not without purpose.

Later, when I was alone, I pondered the other words *grace-filled* and *straight-forward*. I wondered what they meant. Like the word *courageous, graceful* or *grace-filled* was not a description many would use to describe me. I tend to be more like a bull in a china shop. *Straightforward* was rather perplexing also. I had always been scared of hurting someone's feelings. Because of that fear, I would never come right out and say anything directly. Then I had a revelation—a whisper from my Maker. *I created you to be a communicator, a courageous leader whose words would be straightforward but filled with grace.* My heart almost burst. That is who I wanted to be. My soul recognized the truth, and instantly, I chose to believe it.

I was so excited over the revelation produced in my name that suddenly, I wanted to *be* courageous, grace-filled, and direct. I loved this new identity! Remember our lesson from the previous chapter? What you *believe* produces *feelings* that result in how you *behave*. The formula was working for me. When I believed these new words about me, they produced feelings of confidence that were about to erupt into new positive behaviors in my life. I could not wait to be me, but I also wanted everyone I knew to experience the same thing. Because of that, I became curious about the names of the people in my life who I loved. Revelation continued as I researched my family and friends' names. I was shocked at how the definitions of their names represented many facets of their personalities.

I found my father's name incredibly appropriate: Charles, a mighty warrior. He is a mighty warrior, but I had married one as well. My husband is Charles Michael. Michael is a fierce warrior angel, per the Bible. Both men have a strong, fighting spirit that will never allow them to quit, turn tail, or run. They both have infused, inspired, and encouraged me to be me with their love, courage, and tenacious spirits.

I was amused, but not surprised, that all my sons, Steven Austin, Michael Dean, and Benjamin Kemp, also have champion, victorious, or warrior descriptions to one of their names. They are strong young men who do not give up easily. When I studied their other name, it was unique to them alone and very appropriate. One is a peace-filled green valley, another is called beloved, and the other is royal or regal. I was fascinated by how accurately their names described aspects of their personalities.

My middle name, Lee, is translated as "a green valley or a place of rest," which is my favorite color and my favorite place in the world. It is also the same meaning as the names of my beloved great-grandfather, grandfather, aunt, and middle son—*Dean*. Being in their presence is like walking beside still waters near a green valley. My mom and niece's name Janey means "God is gracious." It is true! My mom is one of the most gracious human beings on this planet. Her middle name is Lucy, meaning "bringer of light." Everyone in my family would agree that my mom is a gracious light bearer in each of our lives. Again, I was wowed by the meanings of our names and their role in our identity.

Now it is your turn. Have you ever searched for the meaning of your name? Are you intrigued? Many books and websites give the origin and definition of names. You'll need to be diligent; dig for the root meaning of your entire name. Some of us receive immediate revelation about our names and identities, but I have met others where the correlation was not so obvious. Do not be discouraged if this is the case when you search for the meaning of your name. Consult your Creator to determine if your name can give clues to your unique identity and world-changing destiny.

When your name is called, hear the hidden whisper of your Maker.

You are known. You are loved. You belong. You were planned.

This should fill you with wonder. I challenge you to believe and agree.

CHAPTER 7

Body Work

*Y*ou are a unique and complex creature. You are extraordinary. You consist of three different but distinctive parts. Body. Soul. Spirit. Together they make up the whole of you. To be and do all you were created to, these three parts—your body, soul, and spirit—need time, attention, and care to be healthy. Understanding all parts of *you* is essential for being and doing all you were created to. In the next three chapters, you'll carefully explore yourself, embarking on your own identity boot camp. I think you're ready for this, don't you? This exercise in loving yourself is imperative for successful water walkers, giant slayers, and history makers.

Let us start with carefully assessing our bodies—the tangible, outward part of who we are. The part of us that is recognizable that you can see and touch. It includes but is not limited to our eye color, the color and texture of our hair, our height, our shape, and our weight. It includes our organs, muscles, cells, and bones. Each body is an amazing, unique, and fascinating creation. However, not all of us love our bodies, and because of that, we don't take care of them.

I recognize that this is a sensitive subject. You have the courage to face the truth; I know you do. You are a water walker, giant slayer, and history maker in the making. You can do it. Do not quit now. This may be the most important truth you receive because what you believe about your body may or may not be true, but your feelings are produced by that belief. If negative, they could be causing you unhealthy habits or behaviors. We won't start by discussing those, though. Instead, we will start by determining if the core narrative you have about your body is based on truth or a lie. If we are to be and do all we were created to, we must be honest about our bodies. We need truth. However, we need the truth that does not come from TV, magazines, or our culture. Those views are grossly distorted—not truth.

We were formed in our mother's womb. It was an optimal place for growth. Everything we needed to survive and thrive was there. After we were born, others cared for our bodies, and as we grew older, we were taught to do the same. Eventually, it became our responsibility to take care of ourselves, to be good stewards of this incredible gift we have been given—our bodies. When we were young, it was much easier.

If you grew up going to church, you could not have missed the sermons on being good stewards of our lives and our money. I did not. However, I do not remember lessons from the pulpit on being a good steward of my body. There were sermons on the danger of smoking, alcohol, and drugs, but they had nothing to do with my being healthy. I was told not to have sex before marriage, but I do not remember anyone preaching on exercising more and eating less if I was to be and do all I was created to.

As I became older, my body image was dictated by movie stars and models. I believed that to be beautiful, I must be thin. Thus began my lifelong rollercoaster ride of trying to look like people on television or the movie screen. My health was never once a consideration. It was all about the size of my jeans until I began to contemplate my identity and destiny.

Eventually, during this journey of purpose, I was faced with the question, "How in the world am I ever going to carry out my purpose if I am tired, lethargic, and overweight?" My answer came quickly and simply—I cannot. I had to learn to see my body as a vehicle to my destiny.

Friends, please hear my heart on this. I am not talking about the issues about our bodies that we have no control over, such as genetics. I am talking about the things we do have control over—diet, exercise, and sleep—and the choices we make in those areas. On my journey, I had to take ownership of those choices. Again, I found it much easier to change my unhealthy behaviors if I examined my beliefs and any experiences that caused them. I am five feet, five inches if I stand up very tall. I have what "they" call a muscular build. I am never going to be a willowy supermodel. My age alone would be a deterrent to a modeling career.

We cannot and will not be able to do all we were created to until our bodies are healthy and operating at optimal performance for our age. We need to consult our doctors as well as our Creator. We need to take courage and be honest. It is common to talk about and even condemn those who use excessive amounts of alcohol or take drugs. However, we seem to avoid talking honestly about the abuse of overeating and exercising too little. Doctors are very concerned, telling us repeatedly that we are an overweight society and ignoring the fact will kill us. Please, again, hear my heart. I am not addressing this issue to make anybody feel bad or hurt anyone's feelings. I am addressing this issue because I believe your body and health can keep you from embracing your true identity and fulfilling your destiny. This subject must be addressed directly. Too much is at stake, but I promise to do it gently and gracefully. Remember, I am your biggest fan!

I do not want to shift from being your identity and destiny coach and encourager to being your weight loss coach. This chapter is not about weight. It is about having the strength and stamina to do all God has called you to. If you don't examine your health, just like our beliefs, this issue can give you a false identity and has the power to rob you of your destiny. I believe this struggle affects more of us than excessive alcohol or drug abuse does. We know the health risks associated with those. However, we need to educate ourselves on the health risks associated with not making healthy choices with our nutrition and exercise. Take courage! At the very least, you are not living life as you were created to, and at worst, you are shortening your life span considerably.

Consider that if you are overweight, you are more likely to develop health problems, such as heart disease, stroke, diabetes, certain types of cancer, gout (joint pain caused by excess uric acid), and gallbladder disease. Being overweight can also cause problems such as sleep apnea (interrupted breathing during sleep) and osteoarthritis (wearing away of the joints). The heavier you are, the more likely you are to have health problems. Weight loss can help improve the harmful effects of being overweight. And while many overweight people have difficulty reaching their healthy body weight, studies show that you can improve your health by losing as little as ten to twenty pounds.[5]

This is great news! Yes, being overweight can cause health problems, but you can immediately improve the harmful effects by losing some of the weight. That is truth. Agree with it. Believe it.

Confession

When I was writing this book, I was *moderately overweight*, according to my doctor, heading to *slightly obese* if I did nothing. These words could have quickly become more labels and core narratives that caused negative emotions, which would have turned into self-limiting behaviors if I had accepted them and done nothing. I had to treat them as a diagnosis and not a label. I was immediately encouraged that only a slight loss in weight could improve my physical health and reduce my chance of disease. Stepping on a scale made me feel bad and produced negative actions. Signing up for boot camp—fitness boot camp—made me feel strong and encouraged me to make choices that improved my health.

My weight has rollercoastered for years, but there was only a ten to fifteen-pound variance—until I reached my fifties, and that number became an alarming thirty to forty pounds. When the number was low, my self-esteem was high. When the number was high, my self-esteem was low. I have wrestled with this since I quit smoking in 1994. I decided twenty years ago to stop slowly killing myself in that particular way. It was a good decision, but I received a new problem. Since I did not smoke, the food tasted so much better! Therefore, I ate more. I am not an emotional eater. My problem is that I am a Southerner, and we just like our food fried with *lots* of butter.

In my home, I am the cook, so I cook what I like. I cannot understand why you would spend any time cooking something that does not taste good. Therefore, each night I was confronted with a plate full of food that I love, prepared just the way I like it. Sadly, each night my family of men got up from the table, and I was left there buttering just one more piece of cornbread. When I dared to look at what a "normal" portion is, I was shocked at the small portion of food "they" expected me to live on.

I hated this struggle. I still do! I hate feeling so defeated in this area of my life. I needed new beliefs and agreements if I was going to live out my destiny.

Here is a truth I had to admit and then believe. In this area of my life, I could not do it alone. I needed discipline and accountability. Weighing myself alone only produced negative feelings and bad behaviors. I needed someone to hold me accountable for my choices. You may too. It does not matter if it is Jenny Craig, a fitness boot camp, a personal trainer, Weight Watchers, or one of the numerous other weight loss programs out there. If you do not have the money for those, enlist a friend to exercise with and "weigh in" together regarding your results. Yes, that means letting another person see and record the number on the scale. I am not terribly fond of this disclosure, but I love the results. It works.

My old mistaken core belief raised its ugly head whenever I contemplated accountability in this area of my life. I felt that icky embarrassed feeling in the pit of my stomach every time I publicly weighed in. However, now I confront the old erroneous belief and lie: *I am an embarrassment.* I now scream, "No, I am not!" I was unhealthy at that weight, that is true, but I had the power to make choices to change it. The truth quickly produced feelings of wellness that surrounded me. I could succeed. I also realized the truth that no one else really cared how much I weighed. They were much more concerned about their own weight. Disclosing my weight to others took courage, but my accountability partners encouraged and cheered for me when I did. They celebrated my successes, challenged my choices, and gave me a swift kick in the butt when I needed it. They believed in me when I did not believe in myself. I wanted to be healthy. I wanted to feel strong. To do that, I embraced and included others in that part of my journey. I did not want anything to keep me from discovering my true identity and fulfilling my destiny. That was my motivation!

Living Your Destiny

My dad is an amazing example of someone who took care of their body so they could do the work God called them to. As I type these words in 2023, my dad is eighty-five. In 2007, when he retired at sixty-nine years of age, he went to Africa at my request to help plant a garden at an orphanage in Zambia. What began as one trip became an annual one until 2020 when Covid hit the world. During those thirteen years, he went to Zambia, Tanzania, Malawi, and Uganda with a side trip to the Philippines. He has built a church by hand, started a sewing center, opened a medical clinic, planted so many gardens I have lost count, dug water wells (again by hand), created a feeding program for widows, walked miles in the bush, slept in mud huts, and hiked up mountains, just to fulfill what he believes is his purpose. To do this, he must take a twenty-six-hour flight from Jackson, Mississippi, to the continent of Africa. Once he gets there, he prefers to sleep on a dirt floor in an African hut deep in the bush. He rides for hours in the back of a gravel truck to get to his destination instead of renting a car. He squats over a hole in the ground for a toilet, and he eats food that the FDA has not approved. He even hiked to the top of Mt. Kilimanjaro at the age of seventy-three—taking the shortest and hardest route up. Nineteen thousand feet!

My dad can do all of this because he has taken care of his body every day of his life. He has practiced and continues to practice good stewardship of his body. Those widows and orphans in Africa need him to be and do all he was created to so they can eat. What if he could not go? What if he was not physically able to do what he has been called to do? The answer is quite simple: widows would starve, pregnant women would not have medical care in the bush, and at-risk youth would not have skills for employment.

This mind-boggling statement can apply to all of us. If we are not being and doing what we were created to be and do, there is an unmet need and an unanswered prayer in this world.

My friends, not only is your Creator eagerly awaiting you to be you, but so are other people. My dad's ability to make these trips to Africa is a direct result of how he cares for the body he has been given. He exercises, watches what he eats, gets plenty of rest, and does not put unhealthy things in his body. It is not complicated, but it does take mindfulness, discipline, and accountability, at least for me.

I could spend the rest of the chapters in this book coaching you on physical health. We could set goals to achieve a healthy weight and healthy lifestyle. We could set up accountability and motivational exercises. Fortunately, there are numerous weight-loss and exercise programs aimed at addressing our bodies. I urge you to pick one. Do whatever you need to do to get healthy. Make a goal. Get help. Make a careful assessment, find out what you need to be doing, then *just do it!* Determine a start date. Again, I suggest you consult with a doctor if you have not exercised or had a check-up in a while. Medical websites abound and can provide accurate information on beginning a journey to good health.

Some of you may not have a weight problem but have not had a physical in years. Call your doctor. Get your blood work done. Check your blood pressure. Make sure you are as healthy as you can be. If you are in pain, go to the doctor. If you need to have surgery, schedule it.

When I was fifty-two years old, my knees were killing me. I went to the doctor, and he took x-rays and told me arthritis had eaten away all the cartilage in my knees and that I would never run or jump again. I was devastated. I was too young for knee replacements and decided I was also too young to stop running and jumping. I found a new doctor who did a procedure that allowed me to return to the gym sooner rather than later. I continued losing weight, but I am more excited that I am still running and jumping. Second opinions are a beautiful thing.

Ladies, some of you may be suffering from the symptoms of menopause. I have had a terrible time with this issue for the past thirteen years! Scattered thoughts, weight gain, hot flashes, no sleep, and exhaustion continue to plague me—my poor husband. I am fortunate that he is supportive and encouraging during this very difficult time for me. I had so many different people offering me different versions of the truth. I refused to believe I had to spend the rest of my life feeling bad. I confided in friends my age. I saw three different doctors. I tried many different options until I found one that worked for me. You can too. Call your friends, call your doctor, and take supplements or hormones. Do not believe the lie that your life is over. You still have choices. I did for a year, and it changed my life. I went from tired, hot, weak, irritated, and overweight to fit, strong, active, and excited to attend fitness boot camp. Your life is not over. Fight for your health. If I can do it, so can you. Be a good steward of your body. You need it on this journey of purpose.

What is your goal? When will you start? Call your doctor now and set an appointment. Now for the scary part. Call a friend, someone who loves you and believes in you. Tell them of your commitment. Ask them to hold you accountable in a very practical way. Have them call you and ask you if you exercised that day. Keep a food journal and read it to them daily. Text them your beginning weight and measurements. Update them weekly. Find other ways to be accountable to your partner. You *can* have victory in this area of your life! Believe it, and you will begin to feel it. (By the way, saying *I will start tomorrow* or *I will start on Monday* is not a commitment and will not produce results.)

My prayer for you today is that you will have the faith to believe you can have victory in this area of your life. I long for you and me to choose to believe we are fearfully and wonderfully made as we take responsibility for the care and stewardship of our bodies. I want you to have all the strength and energy required to be and do all you were created to be and do.

CHAPTER 8

Soul Talk

*I*t can get rather confusing when we talk about our soul and spirit, the unseen parts of us. Some people use the words *soul* and *spirit* interchangeably. For our purposes, I have separated them. This chapter we will devote to our soul and the next one to our spirit.

When hurting or diseased, our body shows symptoms that require our attention. If we do not respond to those symptoms, our pain gets worse. So does our soul. Like our bodies, our soul needs examination and attention to be healthy. Our soul is more than just our personality; it is also our will, emotions, and feelings. It is our wants, our needs, and values. Your soul is the essence of you. Your soul includes your heart, your mind, and your beliefs. It can be swayed, influenced, and inspired. It is your personality, your likes, and your dislikes. Your soul is all the parts of you that cannot be seen but greatly influence you and your behaviors and choices.

When all aspects of our soul are healthy, we can trust our opinions, assumptions, and feelings as road maps to our destinies. If they are unhealthy, they are suspect and not to be trusted for truth.

When asked to describe "me," I typically respond like this:

I am an extrovert who also loves my "alone" time. I love to talk. I am loud. I love Mexican food. The Blues make me dance. I love to dance. I hate games. I love deep conversations—soul conversations. I love the sun. I hate the cold, but I love to see snow. I choose still, quiet streams over the roar of the ocean. I love trees. I love green. I love to be up high, looking out into wide-open spaces. I love to start and complete tasks, but I hate managing them. I hate structure. I like to stay at home. I love vacations. I love caring for others but don't like being cared for. I am independent to a fault. I would rather decorate my home than my body. I love being with people. I love having people in my home. I love solitude. I love change. I hate to be bored. I am generous. I have child-like faith. I don't complain, nor do I like complainers. I need my family. I value time alone. I treasure authentic relationships.

These are just some parts of me, a glimpse inside my soul.

What about you? Have you ever given much thought to your soul? The "who am I" question? What do you like, and what do you not like? Have you ever made a careful assessment of this part of you? If not, do so now. Ask people who know and love you to describe you in a paragraph, much like I described myself in the one above. This is always a fun and interesting exercise for people. This exercise is not to encourage you to run to others for your identity but to prove how often your self-perception can be clouded by the negative narratives, which for most of us, began in our childhoods. I am hypervigilant in examining my default behaviors. It is an area of intrigue in my own self-assessment. The emotionally healthy people in our lives can often help us spot a negative core narrative buried deep in our souls. They can hold up a mirror in which we can truly see ourselves. A friend of mine recently did that for me.

I have never really struggled with low self-esteem or lack of confidence (except with that whole weight thing), but I am always surprised when someone compliments me or describes me in a positive or flattering manner. For some reason, I *feel* bad instead of good. I *feel* a need to list all my flaws immediately. With their compliment, I *feel* my disclosures would allow them to see that I do not deserve a compliment. I *believe* I do not deserve a compliment. Notice how my feelings were associated with what I believed, and they had nothing to do with truth.

One of my friends pointed out this habit of mine. When I examined my feelings instead of ignoring them, they were the bridge that led me back to a belief that had become a core narrative. I discovered my brain, unbeknownst to me, was rewinding the tape of my lie back to when I was ten years old, walking down the hall to the principal's office. Though this was a default reaction with no conscious or intentional thought on my part, I still felt the emotions associated with the belief that I had done something wrong, which produced the assumption that I did not deserve compliments. I did not even realize that my brain was looking for every failure, fault, and bad decision I had ever made as evidence. Embarrassment was the feeling that produced the conclusion that I was not special but flawed. I was aware of none of this except that I instantly *felt* bad, and those feelings produced the default behavior or deflecting habit I had acquired. Those feelings had the power to wreak havoc in my life and continued limiting my behavior. The belief that I always did something wrong could have robbed me of my destiny. I would have never attempted the water-walking, giant-slaying feats I was created for if I had allowed the belief to remain.

You see, feelings are subjective. They come from thoughts that can be negative or positive, truths or lies. They come from circumstances, experiences, and interactions with others, many of whom do not know their own identity and destiny. Feelings can change in an instant, depending upon many variables. I was giving more weight to my feelings than they deserved. I incorrectly viewed them as truth.

Do you want to base your identity on something everchanging? I know I don't.

This one issue—your feelings—can hold you captive in a cell of self-doubt from which you will never escape, or they can be a bridge leading you back to a forgotten experience that became a belief and negative core narrative. But I want to remind you that it is who we are, not what we feel, that is important.

Dear mighty warriors and righteous girlfriends, we should never base our beliefs, our truth, and certainly not our choices or actions on our feelings! Yes, we are emotional beings; we all "feel." However, to base your value, self-worth, and choices on your feelings is a recipe for disaster and may have nothing to do with truth.

If we are ever to live out our destinies, we must stop giving so much weight to our feelings. When you begin this journey of identity and destiny, you will not "feel" like you are a water-walking, giant-slaying, history-making person. You first have to choose to believe it and begin acting out of that belief. As I study this topic of emotions and feelings, I am convinced and have seen overwhelming evidence that we have the power to make choices despite how we feel.

We can choose.

The Impact of Feelings on Your Soul

"I don't feel like it!" a teenager shouts at his parent. "You hurt my feelings," a woman accuses her husband. "I feel worthless," a man confesses after losing his job. "I feel useless," an elderly woman prays. I feel, I feel, I feel. As I type those words, I smile, imagining a three-year-old in the midst of a temper tantrum, kicking and screaming as intense emotions erupt and feelings overflow uncontrollably. Emotions can be defined as simply "strong feelings."[6] We give great weight to our *feelings*—too much, I would argue. If we are not careful, our feelings can keep us from being and doing all that we were created to be and do.

When I speak on this topic, I start by asking the audience this question: "How many of you have had your feelings hurt today?" Over half the audience consistently raises their hands; typically, the majority are females since I speak to large groups of women.

Yes, we women are guilty of slinging these words around for real and imagined offenses, which can range from "You forgot my birthday!" to "You didn't like my spaghetti sauce." "You never send me flowers." "You didn't notice I lost weight." I must confess I used "You hurt my feelings" early in my marriage to manipulate my husband. Yes, I said *to manipulate*. To be honest, I somehow felt empowered when I could cause my husband to grovel on occasion for what I deemed was his lack of sensitivity.

What I did not realize at the time was that I was *choosing to be offended*. That bears repeating. I was choosing to be offended, although I did not realize it. Ninety-nine percent of the time, my husband was not trying to be hurtful; he just wasn't particularly sensitive. I did not stop to assess why I was feeling the way I was because I was fixated and determined to make him responsible for my feelings. When he refused, I resorted to pouting for days, hoping he would figure out why I was so hurt and mad. He never did, which hurt my feelings even more. Sometimes it went on for so long that I could not remember why my feelings were hurt in the first place. It all sounds ridiculous, even to my ears. But emotional blackmail is much more than that. It is deadly, and it is wrong. It kills intimacy. It kills unity. It destroys relationships and even marriages. It incites division, causes separation, and will keep us all from our water-walking destiny.

By consulting my Creator and examining my emotions, I learned to be responsible for them instead of placing them on my husband, friends, children, or colleagues. While sharing your feelings with someone you trust can be incredibly healing, be careful not to hit them over the head or make them responsible for them. They are yours alone. No human being or circumstance can *make* you feel anything. Your brain is doing that. Your belief and your assumptions are doing that.

I am not saying this process is easy, but it is necessary if we are to be and do all we were created to. I realize some of these emotions and the circumstances that produce these feelings are strong and scary. We prefer ignoring, numbing, or pretending they are not there over examining them. We actually have the power in our souls to choose to do just that. It is called denial. However, this strategy is a ticking time bomb that will lead to an explosion. Explosions are not good. We get hurt, and the people we love can get hurt. Share your feelings. Examine your emotions. Don't just bury them. Feel them.

I know many women, men, and teenagers dealing with real oppression, depression, and hideous circumstances. Their emotions are real, overwhelming, and debilitating. If this is you, I encourage you to contact a professionally-trained counselor or therapist to help you confront and deal with your emotions and determine your beliefs and experiences that may be causing them. Get help for your pain. Chemical imbalances in our brains can intensify existing emotions or even produce feelings we alone cannot associate with an experience or belief. My encouragement is to get help and get healthy. This is loving yourself and dealing with your emotions in a healthy way. It is *your* responsibility, not that of the people in your life.

Care for your soul. Confront your emotions. Challenge your beliefs. Courageously take your feelings to your Creator and let Him bathe them in His love and truth. Let Him reveal your incorrect beliefs and assumptions—about yourself or the situation you find yourself in. He promises to be bigger than both. As your Creator examines your soul, He will begin to show you and your future. You will discover that your dreams and destiny are much larger than your present circumstances and any feelings associated with them. God will reveal you to you. When you choose to believe, your feelings will slowly change even if your circumstances do not. Resolve daily to think about these things. Don't let your dreams die within you.

I have a theory. Most of us fall into one of two camps with this issue of emotions and feelings. Either we are "feeling-givers," or we are "feeling-takers." I am a feeling-taker. You do not have to ask me to take your feelings; I will come looking for them.

For most of my life, I have assumed responsibility for other people's feelings. My emotions produced my false belief. I hate seeing the people I love in pain. I hate someone being mad at me. I believe it is my fault. We feeling-takers are also called "people-pleasers." I believed incorrectly that it was my responsibility to fix people and their problems, assume their emotions, and be responsible for their happiness. There is a label for people like me—codependent. (Ouch!) That isn't healthy, either!

Like false identities bestowed upon us by others, taking on other people's feelings is exhausting. It is like taking a suitcase full of rocks from everyone you meet all day. It gets heavier and heavier. However, the alternative in my mind was that the people I loved were left feeling bad, sad, or mad—at me. This made me feel bad. So, I behaved in a way that would change my emotions so I could feel good. However, it never lasted because people do not stay happy for long when they do not assume responsibility for their actions. They are always looking for someone to blame or cast off their emotions. I found that people liked it when I assumed responsibility for their feelings. During my soul assessment, my Creator helped me realize that it takes an incredible amount of energy and focus to control my own emotions. Therefore, it is impossible for me to be responsible for my emotions and others' emotions. He showed me that if I continued down this path, I would never be who He created me to be and fulfill my destiny. Sadly, neither would those whom I loved. My greatest desire was to have the courage to be me daily, nothing more but absolutely refusing to settle for anything less while encouraging everyone who crossed my path to do the same. My behaviors were limiting that possibility. I vowed to change. I accepted this truth, and it set me free.

I came to realize that if I am living from my true identity, taking steps toward my water-walking, giant-slaying, history-making destiny, then there will be times when people's feelings will be hurt. They will be disappointed by my actions or inactions. Some people may even get mad when I stop putting their feelings above my purpose. I hate that, I really do. It was a hard behavior for me to change. However, the longing to be and do all I was created to became stronger. It was also freeing to know I am only responsible for making choices that lead me to my own identity and destiny. At the same time, I can point others to God for their answers instead of feeling like I have to produce them. This was a novel concept at the time.

I do not need to have all the answers, and I do not have to make everyone happy, nor do you. *This is not our purpose.* It is unhealthy for our souls. If you tend to be a feeling-taker like me, you may have to repeat this new truth several times a day before you can believe it, feel it, and act out of it. Write it on your five-by-seven cards.

Not relating? Then you may be a feeling-giver. You love us feeling-takers. You may not even realize that you are looking for people to give your feelings to. While sharing your feelings with someone is good and healthy, it is wrong to make them feel responsible for your emotions and happiness. It is wrong to blame another person or even a circumstance for your feelings. This is manipulation. (Ouch!)

Each of us *must* take responsibility for our own emotions and feelings. We must resolve not to be controlled by them—or worse, blame others. Feelings do not come from people. Our feelings come from our beliefs and agreement around an experience. Therefore, we can control them by examining the belief producing them. That is how we change them.

You can choose not to be offended. You can choose to forgive. You can choose to examine your emotions and take them to your Creator. The choice is yours.

Needs, Wants, and Values

Your soul has unique needs, wants, and values. Identifying them is part of carefully assessing yourself, another step in your identity boot camp.

There is no one else like you. You are an exceptional work of art. You are special, unique, and original. If all that is true, why do we strive so hard for most of our lives trying to look and act like everyone else? We spend more time attempting to reinvent ourselves than we do getting to know ourselves. That is just plain wrong! It is critical that *you* know *you*, love *you*, and value *you* so that *you* can be and do all you were created for!

Have you ever considered what you need to get out of bed every day? What do you need to motivate you to be and do all you were created for? What do you need to have in place for you to do your best, never quit, and never give up? What do you need to fight for your true identity and destiny?

What about your wants? What do you want out of life? What do you want to be your legacy? What do you want to be when you grow up? What do you want people to say about you after you leave this planet?

Have you ever considered what you value? What is most important to you in life? What is nonnegotiable and why?

Needs, wants, and values. Knowing these three things about yourself will accelerate your journey to your destiny!

Needs

Needs are conditions, things, and feelings that you *must* have to be satisfied in life—to be content, experience fulfillment, and experience what some would call "finding happiness." Often, needs are the things that must be met before you can really "get on" with life. When we have unmet needs, we tend to get stuck in a rut of a particular behavior or thought pattern and are more susceptible to being sad, depressed, angry, or resentful.

When I say the word *need*, I'm not talking about air to breathe, water, food, shelter, and safety. Of course, we need those to stay alive! I'm talking about the things you "need" to soar. The needs I am talking about are not selfish ones. They are the ones that were crafted and planted in you before time began. They are unique to each of us. It can be acceptance, accomplishments, acknowledgment, compliments, being loved, being needed, being right, having security, clarity, accuracy, comfort, communication, control, responsibility, freedom, peace, order, power, recognition, work, or significance. These things are critical to our motivation, and most of us never contemplate them. Think of your needs as a shot of adrenaline that gets you moving in the right direction.

When these needs are withheld, or we believe they are, we can easily fall prey to despair, disillusionment, depression, disappointment, and discouragement—the Big D's! Left unexamined, our unmet needs can stop us from ever being and doing all we were created for. I encourage you to add this to the list of things to consult your Creator about.

When I began this process, I believed with all my heart that I needed comfort and security to be me. However, during this process of discovering my identity and fulfilling my destiny, I found out those needs were false and had been given importance in my life by culture and society, not my Creator. I had come in agreement with that belief. I incorrectly believed they would keep me safe. However, when I pursued and focused on them, they actually kept me from my destiny. It was so fascinating to discover through consulting my Creator that even my real needs were put within me to help motivate me and propel me to my true identity and destiny.

Here are a few things I discovered about myself. While reading mine, consider what you believe you need to be you and then consult your Creator to see if they are true.

> *I need to matter. I need to know that what I am doing has a purpose and matters in the grand scheme of things. I need to be a part of something bigger than myself. I need to bring people together for a purpose. I need to hear my Creator's voice. I need to lead. I need to speak up. I need the courage to be and do all I am created to do. I need to encourage everyone I meet. I need to be doing something. I need wide-open spaces. I need to be in authentic relationships. I need to try new things. I need to take risks.*

I discovered I needed these things like I need the air I breathe. I needed them to be me. What about you? What do you need to be you?

Wants

Wants are distinct from needs. We are often made to believe that needs are necessary and wants are selfish. I disagree. Wants are conditions, things, or experiences that you feel would optimize your life. Wants can come from past experiences, upbringing, or advertising. Wants, like needs, can be the motivator that gets you out of bed every day! When processed with your Creator, the things you want can give you a glimpse into the destiny you have been created for. Define your wants. Write them down as they come to you. Then dig into the why.

At one point in my life, I thought I wanted to be a mom, a fashion model, a chiropractor, a singer, a home economics major, an interior decorator, and a foreign missionary . . . they all provided clues to the true wants and desires of my heart. Again, I needed to consult my Creator about what He had planted inside me before time began.

I realized from a very young age that I truly wanted to be a world changer. I hate for things to stay the same. I want to be an agent of change. I want to realize my full potential. I want to lead people to their Creator. I want to see lives change. I want to be known. I want to be surrounded by beauty. I want to create something beautiful. I want to leave a legacy for my children, grandchildren, and great-grandchildren in which my ceiling becomes the floor of their life. I want people to say that my life, my journey, encouraged them on their journey. I want to do something that no one has ever done before in a way that no one has done it. I want my Creator to get all the credit. I want you to read this book and begin your journey of discovering your true identity and fulfilling your destiny.

I don't want to miss out on anything God has planned for me, and I don't want you to miss out on what He has planned for you, either.

Values

Values are strong foundational beliefs that anchor our lives. They are the things that matter most to us. They are the nonnegotiable characteristics that best describe who we are and what we live for. They are important to our souls.

Think about where you spend most of your time and effort. When are you the happiest and most fulfilled? Examine what frustrates you. Frustration can sometimes show you where your life is out of balance and how you need to make time for the things you value. Here are some words to get you thinking about what you might value:

Did any of the words jump off the page at you? Highlight them, circle them, or write them down in your journal. Contemplate the *why* of them. This exercise was so difficult for me when I first attempted it. I spent most of my time staring at the words. What *did* I value? I spent so much of my life pleasing everyone else that I was not even sure what I valued, what mattered the most to me.

When I reread the list, I got hung up on picking words I *should* pick, things I believed I should value if I were a good person. Honesty. Peace. Service. Going to church. Whew! My head was spinning. Consulting my Creator was mandatory for even figuring out what I value, for what He created me to value. I discovered that mine are unique to me and will lead me to my destiny. Yours will, too. Here are the top things I value.

Authentic Relationships

My number-one core value is authentic relationships with my Creator and the people in my life. I discovered I have no time for chitchat, small talk, or mindless conversations! I want to know my Creator and the people I love deeply. I want to know them and be known by them. I do not have time for anything else.

Years ago, I would have defined my values as God, family, and others—all relationships. While that is still true, I learned they must be deep. I have been designed with a large capacity for relationships: deep, meaningful, direct, and authentic relationships. Those types of relationships are critical to my identity and destiny! I need purpose in everything, even in my relationships. I discovered that this is why I hate to play games. I would rather have deep, meaningful conversations instead. You may have described this value as communication. You are right. I love to talk!

Marriage and Family

I value my marriage and my family. Sounds trite, huh? Most of us would list our family as something we value—or at least believe we should. However, the way I value them is a bit different. In my StrengthsFinder 2.0 results, I am called a maximizer. If something is good, I want it great; if it is great, I want it grand; if it is grand, I want it grandiose! I love bigger and better. Relationally, I am the same. I want more from my marriage, more from that relationship, more for and from my husband and our kids. I want us all to be better because of each other. I want my Creator to use our family to change the world. My greatest fear is that, individually or collectively, they will settle for less than they were created for. (Yes, I drive all of them crazy!)

Growing

I value growing and learning because I know it is necessary to reach my full potential. Then I want to replicate, duplicate, and impart everything within me. I hate being bored. I want to be stimulated. I want to feel alive, and through my times of intimacy with my Creator, I was shown this is an important part of my destiny—to be fully alive, growing daily, and producing "fruit" that lasts an eternity. Without consulting my Creator day by day, I do not think I would have been able to state this as a value.

At first glance, my life and past did not seem to reflect this value. I did not go to college and did not have a great deal of desire to excel when I was in school. However, my Creator reminded me that I love to read. I devour books. Reading is learning. I love to go to conferences. I love to listen to speakers. I love to hang out with people who are smarter than I am. And though my life choices took me from a path of structured learning, I appeased my hunger for knowledge in a more unstructured way. I long for knowledge that produces personal growth. For years now, I have asked my Creator to be my teacher.

Action

I value doing something, anything—even if it is wrong! I am not scared of failure, but I am scared of sitting by and doing nothing. I hate sitting still. I hate being bored. I hate worrying and wringing my hands. I hate problems with no answers. I like action! It is so affirming when your Creator shows you that the very thing that often drives people crazy about your personality is the very thing placed inside of you to ensure you will fulfill your destiny! It is incredibly encouraging to know that you are created on purpose for a purpose—even if you are often misunderstood or told to sit still.

Solitude and More . . .

Solitude, wide-open spaces, aesthetically pleasing environments, influencing, respect, and responsibility round out the top ten values of my life. I have others that I also try to be intentional about living from, but these are the main ones.

I laughed out loud as I reviewed the words I had written about myself. What a complicated, complex, convoluted individual I am. What was my Creator thinking when He made me? I remember wondering that in the early days of carefully assessing who I was. Today, I see how uniquely I have been crafted on purpose for a purpose.

My needs, my wants, and my values have all become indicators that escorted me to my destiny and motivated me to stay on course. When those are out of balance, I stall. I get stuck. This knowledge has given me clarity in what to say yes to and what to say no to. I can always tell when I have made choices that do not reflect my core values, needs, or wants. I become overwhelmed, irritable, and frustrated.

Aligning these three things—my needs, wants, and values—with how I spend my time is vital to my identity and destiny. This is literally what it means to stay true to yourself. This is what it means for our souls to be healthy. Often, I need to recalibrate my schedule and make sure I am operating out of my values. I need to be kind to my soul.

Assessment Tools

Another way to assess who we are, another mirror we can use to understand our unique souls, is through personality assessments. They offer tangible, objective proof of who you are and your unique strengths, gifts, and talents. They can help you glimpse into your soul. They also can give you a new vocabulary and new truths about yourself.

Hide not your talents. They for use were made.
What's a sundial in the shade?

—Benjamin Franklin

I have listed three of my favorite soul and personality assessments. I highly recommend them to assist you in making a careful assessment of who you are. Two recommendations require you to buy the books to take the assessment. One assessment provides you with a code for an online test, and the other has the assessment in the back of the book. The third assessment I recommend is online and free.

StrengthsFinder 2.0

This is one of my favorite assessment tools. It focuses on your natural strengths instead of your weaknesses; it highlights what you have instead of what you lack. Since I tend to focus on my weaknesses, this assessment was pure delight. Author Tom Rath shows you how to develop these raw strengths into excellence, but you must buy the book to get the code to take the computerized assessment.

> Do you have the opportunity to do what you do best every day? For years I did not and most people I coach or interview say the same thing. All too often, our natural talents, our strengths, go untapped. From the cradle to the cubicle, we devote more time to fixing our shortcomings than developing our strengths.[7]

According to this assessment, I am a wooer, relater, communicator, activator, and maximizer. What a zany soul combination. I had no idea what those words meant. However, they sounded much better than the descriptions I was accustomed to. I eagerly read the details from the report I received. Truth. The words I read were about me. I loved the descriptions of my strengths. Some things I knew about myself, but I would not have called them strengths. I *do* love to *influence* complete strangers by wooing them into deep, meaningful conversations that turn into *relationships* and purpose-filled endeavors. I love *communicating* my passions with my voice or a pen, making quick decisions to advance a plan while *maximizing* individual efforts that will literally and collectively change the world!

The Five Love Languages

Live a life of love. It sounds so simple. When we have been loved well, we can love others well. However, many people have not been loved well by the other humans in their life. That is why our Creator has adopted us into His family—to lavish His love on us so we can lavish it on others. I have discovered that on my own, I do not know how to love others well. How do I love them in a way that speaks to the core of their being?

The answer to this question can be found in Gary Chapman's book *The Five Love Languages*. Knowing your love language and the love language of everyone in your life is the most amazing tool I have found in "loving well." Generally, we tend to love others in the way we long to be loved. In his book, Gary assesses your own love language and teaches how to love others in their language. I highly recommend this book. Every married couple, every parent, and every friend should read this book. It can save relationships.

Mr. Chapman's book explained much about my soul to me, things I did not know about myself. I am a *words of affirmation* girl. Long, deep meaningful conversations are my favorite things in the entire world. I do not need flowers or jewelry—just write me a love letter! I do not need someone to sit and hold my hand or go to the grocery store with me— just send me a text or a tweet and tell me I matter. Words are very powerful to me—both words of praise and words of criticism. One has the power to build me up and the other to tear me down. Now I understand why words are so powerful to my soul.

I discovered in this book that my husband and best friend are *quality time* people. Now everything makes sense in our relationship. They could care less if I write them a three-page letter or spend an hour talking on the phone; to feel loved, they need to spend time with me. This was a revelation that strengthened our relationship. I am now intentional about scheduling time to be with them so I can love them well. They also love me by writing me a note or indulging my need for long, late-night conversations.

The Enneagram

Another of my favorite assessments is the Enneagram. It is a tool that has been particularly valuable to me in understanding myself and my default reactions. The assessment can be found online at The Enneagram Institute. Here is an excerpt from their website:

> From one point of view, the Enneagram can be seen as a set of nine distinct personality types, with each number on the Enneagram denoting one type. It is common to find a little of yourself in all nine of the types, although one of them should stand out as being closest to yourself. This is your basic personality type. Everyone emerges from childhood

with one of the nine types dominating their personality, with inborn temperament and other prenatal factors being the main determinants of our type. This is one area where most all of the major Enneagram authors agree—we are born with a dominant type. Subsequently, this inborn orientation largely determines the ways in which we learn to adapt to our early childhood environment. It also seems to lead to certain unconscious orientations toward our parental figures, but why this is so, we still do not know. In any case, by the time children are four or five years old, their consciousness has developed sufficiently to have a separate sense of self. Although their identity is still very fluid, at this age children begin to establish themselves and find ways of fitting into the world on their own.[8]

I am fascinated by the Enneagram because it talks so much about identity. The Enneagram was a tool for me to see the contradictions of my soul and my personality and the danger of not being aligned with the purposes and plans I was created for.

Have you made a soul search? Do you know what you need to be you? Have you assessed your wants and defined your values? Take the time to make a careful assessment of who you are. Consult your Creator about the needs, wants, and values placed inside you before time began, and get rid of the ones that are not part of who you are. You will feel so free. You will be ready to fly on the wings of eagles and reach your destiny.

CHAPTER 9

Your Eternal Identity

*Y*our spirit is the eternal essence of you. It's the part of you that will remain when your body is gone. Your spirit knows and recognizes truth that does not need an explanation. It requires no words to communicate. This is the part of you that was known by your Creator before time began.

Our need to be known, our need to matter, to belong and make a difference, is strong within our souls. I believe our souls ask, "Who am I?" and "Why am I here?" Our spirits hold the answers to those questions. I believe that before time began, our Creator planted those answers inside our spirits and waits for us to ask these questions.

There is a verse in the Bible that says, "Before I formed you in the womb I knew you, before you were born I set you apart" (Jeremiah 1:5 NIV). When I ponder these words, I am intrigued. Before I was formed, I was known. Before I was born, I was set apart for a purpose. This concept defies logic, but somewhere inside of me, deeper than my soul and the logic within my brain, I agree. I hear these words and immediately believe; I want to believe. The belief that I am known intimately, set apart for a purpose, and created exactly right produces emotions in me that causes me to take steps that will propel me into my destiny. I reject the belief that some hold, that we are finite, expendable, and unplanned creatures. Those words do not make me feel like I can change the world. Those words do not make me feel I have a purpose. I choose not to believe them. My spirit rejects those words as truth. Trusting your spirit, your gut, that still small voice inside you, requires practice. It often requires we shut off our brains and stop being logical to hear, truly hear, the Spirit-to-spirit conversations within us.

Spirit-recognized Truth

Your spirit knows truth. Your spirit recognizes truth. Our Creator speaks to our spirit about *who* we are and *what* we are supposed to be doing! That is happening deep within us. It totally blows me away. It is just too big for my soul (my mind) to comprehend, but in my spirit, I recognize it as truth. Let me give you an example of your spirit responding separately from your soul.

Have you ever been moved to tears over pure beauty—the beauty of an evening sunset that lit the sky with brilliant colors or a waterfall cascading down the face of a mountain, spraying a mist that was a multi-colored prism of rain? Perhaps it was when you watched your child sleeping and a smile spread across his mouth, leaving you to wonder what he was dreaming about. Maybe it was a specific melody of music or the words of a song that cut straight to your core by describing feelings or thoughts you recognized but could not have articulated. Was it a time you saw pure innocence in the eyes of a child? Did your tears surprise you? Sunsets, waterfalls, music, lyrics, babies, and beauty all travel past the logic of our souls and go straight to our spirits, communicating a truth we recognize but cannot name with mere words.

The emotions or feelings we sense are not filtered through a belief. The scenarios go past our soul and logic, speaking to our spirit, suggesting we are incredible creatures, more than accidents, connected to creation and others. They communicate that we are eternal beings with eternal purposes. Beauty, music, and babies cause a wonder inside us that is difficult to contain or explain. When my Creator speaks to me, I feel the same way. Tears come to my eyes as my spirit recognizes truth my soul often cannot—that my Creator has a great love and a unique destiny planned for me before time began. I am a part of something so much bigger than myself. I need to be me. Our spirits are tuned to a different frequency. It requires we get alone. Walk in nature. Touch the earth— barefooted. Climb a mountain. Listen to music. Paint a picture. Create a space for divine communication—Spirit to spirit with our Creator. It is a place of divine favor where blessings are bestowed freely and lavishly. The communication is between my Creator and the essence of me. It is hard to explain, but my spirit alone recognizes this truth. Quickly, I must choose to believe it before my soul, my logical brain, or other human beings try to distort its melody. I choose to trust the divine dialogue going on inside of me and wooing me to my identity. Like our bodies and souls, this part of ourselves must be given attention, or we will never tap into the frequency or crack the code.

Of our three parts, our spirits receive the least amount of our attention. Our bodies are fed daily, and rightly so, because if we did not eat, we would die. Our souls are constantly being fed a diet of our wants. "I want what I want when I want it." We are selfish creatures with a vested interest in meeting our needs and wants. However, our spirits do not demand. Our spirit, the eternal essence of who we are, longs to dialogue with our Creator in a place where we learn to recognize and trust the eternal truth about ourselves. Time must be carved from our busy lives to gaze upon the beautiful, the mystical, the grand, and the unexplained in our world. We must feast upon our Creator's words that penetrate our souls and pierce our spirits with truth. Our soul inquires, *Who am I?* Our Creator responds, *You are mine. You are called beloved. You have a place to belong. You are planned, created on purpose for a purpose. You have a water-walking, giant-slaying, history-making destiny. You will change the world.*

This inner dialogue with our Creator creeps past our logic and provides a peace that surpasses all understanding. It comes in times of solitude, which most of us run from. We must become comfortable being alone with ourselves and just our Creator. It is a place where no other person can journey with you because it is inside you. This place is where we first claim our identity and vow to fulfill our destiny. It is where we first recognize the truth about who we are and what we are created to do. It is a place where we discover we are seen for exactly who we are, and despite everything we have done, we are loved completely and unconditionally.

When my Creator asked me, "Do you have the courage to be you, the you I created?" along with the concept, "You were created on purpose for a purpose," I wrestled with them for about three years. I was doing everything I have encouraged you to do—assessments, getting alone, examining my beliefs, checking items off like a things-to-do list. I was making so many exciting discoveries about my identity, I just knew I was getting close to discovering my destiny! I was working on getting healthy in my body and soul while trying to tap into the spirit, the most elusive part of this journey. That is until my birthday, the same day I discovered I was born on my great-grandmother's birthday when I had an experience that I can only describe as extraordinary. I didn't write about this experience in the original edition of this book because it was so private and personal to me. I have shared it in intimate places but not very often. Twenty years after the experience and for the tenth anniversary edition of this book, I've decided to share it with you.

Bear with me, as it is hard to put into words what actually happened.

I was in my car. It was my birthday. I was going to pick up my blouse from the alterations shop. I wasn't praying. I wasn't doing anything you could call spiritual. I was excited to go to dinner and dance with my husband that evening. There was a song on the radio, but I wasn't paying attention to it because the volume was so low. I wasn't singing along. Suddenly, and I mean suddenly, it was as if someone reached into my car and turned up the volume on my radio. The music filled my car, surrounding me like a physical presence as the lyrics pierced my soul and spoke to my spirit in a deep way. At the same time I was driving, I *saw* myself in the outfit I had planned to wear that evening, dancing with a man in a tuxedo. I never saw His face, but I knew Him instantly. He was familiar to me. I had believed in Him for most all of my life. It was Jesus. I *watched* myself, floating across the dance floor, following His lead. (This was pretty incredible in and of itself because I always try to lead when I am dancing, and I am not very graceful.) Deep within me, I had always wanted to dance like that, to be held like that, to feel like that—the most important person in the world to another.

If you've ever heard the song "Hungry" by Kathryn Scott, it was not a favorite song of mine at the time. I may have heard it before at church. As the dance continued, the song continued to penetrate my spirit, inviting me to dance with my Creator and be known in a way I have never experienced. I didn't know the lyrics by heart, but my spirit must have because I started sobbing. I had to pull my car off to the side of the road because I couldn't see anything but me, this man, and the dance.

There were no audible words spoken, but I could hear. I could feel. I knew. I was suddenly exposed and completely vulnerable in a way I had never been. People say that when you are dying, your life passes before you. That was similar to what I was experiencing. Every secret I had hidden, every thought I had not spoken, every word I had, every selfish choice I had made was laid bare. I was laid bare. I felt deeply, but it was what I should have felt with this surgical exposure. It wasn't guilt, shame, or regret—no! It was the complete opposite. I felt completely known and loved in a way I have never experienced. It was liquid love. Pure unconditional love. It didn't matter what I had done or not done—this love was not based on anything other than who I was. I felt seen. I felt joy. I felt innocence. I felt grace. I felt complete.

Then I heard these words whispered deep inside of me to my spirit.

"This. This is what you have been searching for—this knowledge, this love. This is what

you need in order to truly be and do all I have created you to. My daughter, I created you on purpose for a purpose. You are ready!"

I now knew for the first time what it meant to be a child of God, to be created in His image, for His purpose. His Spirit spoke to my spirit—not in audible words but with the same knowledge of beauty we receive in a sunset, a waterfall, a piece of art, or a score of music. I was sobbing tears of joy for the gift I had received in my car on my birthday at that moment. I wanted it to last forever.

When the music volume lowered as miraculously as it increased, I felt an incredible sense of peace. I sat in the moment, trying to understand what had happened. I had no words, but I was bathed in love. I felt a sense of urgency in my spirit, and a thought popped into my head: "How do I tell others about this?" My first thought was of you! I began praying for everyone I knew and everyone I would ever meet, "Jesus! Dance with them!"

I don't know what you would call this experience. Some may call it a vision, a supernatural experience. I had never had one before and haven't had one since. I didn't literally see Jesus. I didn't audibly hear words. But it was an experience my mind did not create but one my spirit recognized that affected my life greatly. That experience gave me the courage to finally say yes! I wanted to walk on water. I wanted to fly on the wings of eagles. I wanted to fight giants with stones. I wanted to change history.

God says, "You will seek me and find me when you seek me with all your heart" (Jeremiah 29:13 NIV). That is the best way I can describe what happened. I went seeking God, and I also found me.

Identity boot camp is designed to help you discover your identity and provide opportunities to practice and solidify it. Believing in and acting from your true identity guarantees success in your destiny. Practice does make perfect. I want your new identity to become your new core narrative. I want your belief in yourself to be strong and impenetrable. I want you to succeed in your world-changing mission. I want you to dance with Jesus.

CHAPTER 10

Boot Camp Looks and Feels a Lot Like War

*O*nce I was discussing the topic of identity, destiny, and purpose with an army staff sergeant friend before she departed for her third tour of duty in Iraq. I told her I had made a *secret* discovery about the importance of knowing your identity before fulfilling your destiny. She just laughed at my revelation. I was shocked when she told me my secret had been employed by the United States Army for years as a part of new recruit training called boot camp. The U.S. Army's boot camp is where a civilian recruit is transformed into a U.S. Army soldier.

I wanted to learn everything I could about that transformation because I had a sense that it could be critical in learning to embrace my own identity and training others to embrace theirs. In great detail, my friend outlined how much time, effort, and training the army spends in reinforcing a soldier's collective identity as a member of the U.S. Army before they ever divulge that soldier's destiny, their mission.

During the first week of the ten-week boot camp, new recruits receive hours of classroom instruction on the army's heritage, the seven core values of the U.S. Army, the code of military justice, and the soldier's creed. All of this information, combined with weeks of rigorous training, leads to their transformation.

As my staff-sergeant friend talked, I imagined a long line of new army recruits on the first day they report for duty. I can feel their nervousness as they contemplate the unknown. They are so young, probably nineteen or twenty years old— way too young, in my opinion, to sign up to defend our country and possibly go to war. My opinion stems from being a mom who would fear for the lives of her young men. In reality, I would be a proud mom if any of my sons enlisted in the armed forces, just as many have proudly watched as their sons and daughters fought and died for our country and the freedom we have held for hundreds of years. This is a high calling and grand purpose.

These young recruits are all so different when they enlist. They fit no mold. They have diverse educations, aspirations, and experiences. They come from different family environments and histories. Yet they have all signed up for the same thing: to serve their country, to be a part of something bigger than themselves. I admire them. It takes a great deal of courage and faith just to enlist.

Do you think these young recruits know what they have signed up for? Do they really understand what they have committed their lives and futures to? I doubt it. They may have signed up because they want to do something meaningful and purposeful. Maybe they want to be a part of something far bigger than their individual selves. They may have joined to follow family members or continue a family tradition. The reasons may vary for joining, but they all end up in the same place—boot camp. Boot camp is designed to provide these young soldiers with a collective water-walking, giant-slaying, history-making identity and destiny.

Soon after enlisting, I am sure some of these young people may question their decision or even wish they could run back home, while others are gung-ho and eager to begin their journey of purpose. Either way, by enlisting, they have begun a journey of faith—faith in the U.S. Army. They have given up their individual rights and the control of their own lives for the privilege of being identified as a soldier in the United States Army. It is an honor.

The army is responsible for training and transforming these young civilians into soldiers. On the first day of boot camp, do you think the army distributes weapons and discloses missions to these new recruits, sending them out to the front lines with a pat on the back and a *"You can do it!"* cheer? No! Of course not. These new soldiers wouldn't stand a chance. If they did not get themselves killed immediately, they might succeed in getting half their unit blown up. If, on that first day of boot camp, all of those anxious, out-of-shape, untrained recruits were given battle plans without any instruction or sense of what it means to be a soldier in the U.S. Army, chaos and mayhem would ensue, and most would quit or die on the first day they started.

Thus the army has a different plan, a tried and true method—boot camp. Recruits begin an intentional, intensive, and repetitive process designed to teach each new soldier their individual and collective identity as a member of the U.S. Army. While missions are given based on assessments of individual ability, strengths, and aptitudes, the identity of a U.S. soldier is common to everyone who survives boot camp.

Do you think the army lets new recruits define or determine their own identity? Do you think the army polls each new recruit and asks, "What do you think the identity of a soldier should be?" Do they put it out for a vote? Of course not. The army, and only the army, defines the identity of its soldiers. It is constant and does not change. In both word and deed, the army begins the time-honored process of bestowing the new recruits' identity upon them. It is woven throughout the ten weeks of boot camp.

"Treat a man as he is, and he will remain as he is.
Treat a man as he could be, and he will become what he should be."

—Ralph Waldo Emerson

That is what the army does. The army teaches the new recruit who he or she can be. The process cannot be rushed. The army stresses and repeats who they are and how they are expected to behave when bearing their new identity. The bar is high, and the training is intense for this transformation to occur.

It takes time for the army to believe in and trust the recruits' new identity. The officers know it will take a while before their behavior mirrors this new identity. That is why repetition is important. The soldiers memorize and recite, out loud and often, their creed and core values to make the army's belief system and values their own.

The army knows what I have learned: if recruits believe they are U.S. Army soldiers, they will act like U.S. Army soldiers. That is why so much time and money is spent on training, repetition, boot camps, and practice drills—to solidify their identity in such a way that when they are in the middle of their mission, they will never question who they are or what they were trained to do.

The recruit is taught to trust that training. By the time they graduate and leave boot camp, they have become a U.S. soldier. The creed is no longer something they just recite; it is who they are and a part of them. It defines them. It is a statement of their collective identity.

THE SOLDIER'S CREED

I am an American Soldier.

I am a Warrior and a member of a team.

I serve the people of the United States and live the Army Values.

I will always place the mission first.

I will never accept defeat.

I will never quit.

I will never leave a fallen comrade.

I am disciplined, physically and mentally tough, trained and proficient in my warrior tasks and drills.

I always maintain my arms, my equipment and myself.

I am an expert and I am a professional.

I stand ready to deploy, engage, and destroy the enemies of the United States of America, in close combat.

I am a guardian of freedom and the American way of life.

I am an American Soldier.[9]

Notice that this creed has many sentences beginning with *I am*. Those are the identity sentences stressing who they are. The other sentences tend to begin with *I will*. Those sentences reflect the behaviors they have chosen to demonstrate in advance of their circumstances and being given their mission.

I felt like one of those eager, untrained, clueless young recruits when I first said yes to being who I was created to be and fulfilling my destiny. Like them, I had no idea what I had signed up for. I had no idea my life was not my own. I had enlisted for a mission of purpose, not knowing where it would lead or the training it would require. I was both scared and excited. Although I said yes, I was in no way ready for my Creator to reveal His plans for me because I struggled to grasp and act out of my new identity. If I had known what my destiny would entail before fully coming to terms with my true identity, I would have fallen on the floor in laughter. If I would have seen the battles I have been required to fight, I might have quit before I started or turned tail and run for the hills.

In the beginning stages, I was more comfortable with who I was instead of who I was created to be. My past looked like it disqualified me from a future of divine purpose. I had no obvious talents. I talked too much, listened too little, and spoke with a Southern accent while frequently butchering the English language. I write like I talk, hate to leave home, and have no college degree. I have been divorced, despise math, and am frightened to death to try anything I am not good at. Looking at myself through my own eyes, I did not see much potential; my identity screamed mediocrity. Like our young army recruits, I needed to go through an identity boot camp if I was ever going to be who I was created to be, and you will need to do the same.

My Personal Creed

That is what these first chapters were designed to be—the beginning of your identity boot camp. Before the next half of this book, I would like to share a creed I wrote for myself, inspired by the Soldier's Creed. I needed a creed of my own that stated who I was and what I was willing to do. I drafted a powerful statement of identity that I could repeat to myself whenever doubt crept in. Feel free to borrow mine or, even better, consult your Creator and write your own.

MY PERSONAL CREED

I am a beloved child of God.

I am lavished with love.

I am fearfully and wonderfully made.

*I am a masterpiece woven together by God
in my mother's womb.*

*But even before that, I was imagined and
crafted by the God of the universe
on purpose for a purpose.*

Good plans have been designed especially for me.

*I have a destiny that will transform lives,
change history, and answer prayers.*

I am a child of God.

I embrace that identity. I trust in that identity.

*I will not allow anyone else to ever tell me
who I am except my Maker.*

*I will only consult my Creator for
my identity and my destiny.*

*I am a water walker, giant slayer,
and history maker.*

I refuse to quit.

I will change the world.

I will have the courage to be me.

The path to your purpose requires you to embrace your identity. It must be unshakeable. No more self-doubt or low self-esteem. Going through boot camp will make your identity stick. It is designed to make you ready for your water-walking, giant-slaying, history-making destiny.

You need to know that you can trust yourself when the battles come. Believe me, they will come. You need to trust that when things get tough, you will not quit. Your boot camp is designed to test your faith in your Creator. Having said that, I must warn you that on some days, your boot camp will look and feel a lot like war.

Establishing Deep Trust

I have to tell you a secret: no one feels qualified to do what they are created and called to do. I certainly do not on many days. I still feel like the poster child for the ordinary. Boot camp is difficult but a necessary precursor to receiving our marching orders. It is there where we are prepared for our purpose. It makes us better and stronger, and establishes and reinforces our belief in our identity and so much more. Boot camp establishes a deeper trust between you and your Commander.

When my son, Austin, was in the fourth grade, I was asked to teach his Sunday school class. The lesson that day was on trusting our Creator. I wondered all week how to illustrate this lesson in a way that rowdy fourth-grade boys could embrace. I read some inspirational books and pondered several ideas before tossing them out. At the very last minute, I received divine inspiration.

When the boys all arrived at class and finally got settled in their chairs, I asked them to come up and form a line in front of me. I asked Austin to go last. One by one, I asked the boys to stand about two feet in front of me with their backs to me. I then asked the first boy to close his eyes and cross his hands over his chest.

Then, I told him to fall backward.

His eyes flew open, and he turned around, shocked. I repeated the instructions, got him in place again, told him to close his eyes, and again said, "Fall backward."

He could not do it.

Hands flew up, and all fifteen of the other fourth-grade boys screamed, "Let me!" bravely adding, "I can do it!"

None of them could do it. Not a one, except for my son.

Confidently, Austin stood in front of me, back turned, eyes closed, and arms crossed, and with complete trust, he fell back into my arms without hesitation. All the boys cheered. He smiled. He was able to do what the others could not do because he *knew* me. He had experiences with me in which I had been faithful. He had a history and a relationship with me and was able to trust me completely.

Trust cannot be rushed. It is evidence-based. It is established through experience; you could say it is a boot camp-like experience. We learn to trust another person or even a product over time. Trust is birthed from a history of faithfulness. Trust is a peace that settles in our soul and originates from a deep, intimate relationship or knowledge of another. Trust is achieved slowly during the routine daily dialogue of our lives.

The more trust established between two individuals, the more the other person is invited to speak into our lives and circumstances. Trust must be built, which is done when someone consistently follows through with what he or she has said.

Military boot camp exercises and drills are designed for the purpose of establishing and cementing trust between peers and those in authority. Trusting that leaders will do what they say and provide the resources needed to fulfill the mission is critical to success. Boot camp shows us whom we can trust. And it also teaches us to trust ourselves and our training. God's boot camp is no different.

In our lives, we go through boot camp situations beyond our ability to fix and require divine intervention. Delayed answers to prayers, unexpected circum-stances, and problems with no immediate solutions are all exercises and drills used by our Maker to ascertain our level of faith and trust in His leadership and our new identity.

We are competent people. We get up, go to work, earn a paycheck, then drive the car we bought with our hard-earned money to the local store to buy groceries to feed ourselves. We like being independent, problem-solving people. All of these actions are done without any outside help, we proudly claim. On any given day, we can fight fires, save lives, get an education, buy a home, get a job, build a house, paint a picture, invent a device, and have a baby, all without divine intervention. We are wonderfully and fearfully made. However, if we are to attempt world-changing destinies, we are going to have to tap into the divine. We will need to be trained in how and when to attempt the impossible. That is why we need to go through boot camp—to learn to trust our identity, others, and our Creator.

Words in My Spirit

Start an international organization to help people find their purpose—copyright all the materials. You will travel the world. I will give you the financial resources equivalent to Starbucks. You will meet the needs of those in society that no one is meeting. You will build them homes. You will call them family. You will have daughters. You will start Courage Cafés. You will hire the best of the best and pay them marketplace salaries. You will be united as one. You will be of one heart, one mind, and one spirit. You will write a book. You will speak to stadiums full of people. The next generation will take the organization to places you cannot dream of.

All of those words have been whispered to my spirit. Some have come true, and others I am still believing for. When I first heard them, I was filled with wonder and excitement that is difficult to articulate. I had spent so much time cementing my identity that when the words of my destiny were finally revealed, I was overwhelmed by my assignment. While my soul and my logical brain knew I could never attempt to fulfill these on my own, my spirit recognized that this was exactly what I was created to do. I was humbled by that which I was chosen and prepared for. My entire life made sense as those words settled deep within my soul.

When I received my mission, I was reeling from a very intensive boot camp experience designed to solidify my identity and prepare me for this very destiny. All I knew was that boot camp felt a lot like war. On some days, I could not tell the difference. However, when my mission was revealed, I realized my Maker ordained it to prepare me for the future. Through those difficult experiences, I gained a new level of trust in myself and my Creator. How thankful I am for them all. I am still drawing encouragement from them today. Boot camp taught me to trust myself and my Creator at a whole new level.

To fulfill the world-changing destiny assigned to you, you must have complete trust that you are prepared for your purpose. You must have complete trust that the provision of resources will be there for you to succeed. In addition, you must earn the trust of your Maker. He must know that you can be trusted to finish the task He assigns and not quit when things get tough.

Boot Camp Weeds Out Quitters

You have to resolve within yourself before you even start on this journey of purpose that quitting is not an option. I often play mind games with myself to bring clarity to situations. I treat every obstacle, every problem, and every opportunity in my life as either a test to be won or a battle to be fought. Both situations require my commitment to the calling and purpose of my life. Both require that I not quit when things get tough.

The first situation, the test, is designed by my Creator to teach me, test me, or strengthen me. I want to pass, win, or succeed because I know the lesson is required to move me into the strategic position designed for me. It shows what is best for me and fully prepares me for future trials and circumstances. The lesson makes me strong. It teaches me to fight so I am competent and deadly in battle. I want to prove that I will not quit and can be depended upon.

The other battle—the one that tries to rob me—puts steel in my spine, makes me angry, and causes me to fight for and take back what is rightfully mine. I feel much stronger when I see myself as a warrior in battle rather than a victim of my circumstances. Through boot camp and war-like situations, I have been trained to fight. I am confident. I am prepared to face my enemy. I have been guaranteed victory. I will not quit.

In both scenarios, I must resolve not to quit when things get difficult. There is much at stake, and my part is critical to what happens in my world. One of my greatest fears is to realize that I was a day away from victory or promotion, but I gave up and quit one day too soon.

Everything can change in a single day. What if tomorrow is the day everything changes? What if you quit too soon?

Boot camp weeds out the quitters. Before you are given the details of your destiny, you will be put through rigorous situations and war-like circumstances to determine whether you will quit. Boot camp has taught me that winning simply means not quitting. During some of the most difficult days of my life, the only prayer I could utter—through clenched teeth and with tears running down my cheeks—was, *"I will not quit!"* I have resolved, made up my mind in advance, that no matter the test I have been given or the battle I am fighting, I will not quit. What about you?

Obey without Question

In the military, there are clear lines of authority. You learn immediately to say, "Yes, sir!" and not question commands or orders given by your superiors.

An extreme level of trust is required to obey without question. Without that level of trust, a situation can become abusive and destructive. As we talked about previously, boot camp is designed to build that level of trust.

In the family I was raised in, it was exactly the same way. My dad was the head of the household. There were no majority votes or soliciting of opinions.

Everything worked well if we just did what we were told. Now, my dad was not abusive. He was not a dictator. Repeatedly, he demonstrated his love for his family, integrity, and ability to provide for us. He had a vision for our family, and we all had important parts, but at critical and stressful times, he had to know he could depend upon our instant obedience. We were able to do that because we had complete trust in him. Because of his character and love, obeying was easy, even if I didn't have all of my *why* questions answered. I believe our Creator requires the same of us if we are to be and do all our destiny requires.

One morning, I felt these words penetrate to the core of my being: "Sell your house."

What? Are we moving?

Silence followed. It was decision time for me: Do I obey what I have come to trust and what I have learned is the direction of my Creator? After much discussion with my husband and family, we decided to "step out in faith" even though we did not know where we were moving to or what we were supposed to do. Yes, people thought we were crazy. Even I thought so on some days! However, we did as ordered *without* having all our desired answers.

Because I had gone through boot camp, I had proved I could be trusted, and I knew that my Creator could be trusted as well. I had complete faith that my family and I were being strategically moved to where we were supposed to be. I knew this was an exercise in obedience. Would I obey without having all the answers? Trust in my God was being put to the test, one I desperately wanted to pass. I truly believe my destiny hinged on it.

Weeks later, we received a new address to begin the early work of Courage Worldwide, the nonprofit I founded, to build homes and provide resources for children who were recovered from sex trafficking. We would move to Sacramento, CA, where ranch prices were much lower than in the San Francisco Bay Area. My destiny was underway.

Are you in a situation where you do not have all the answers but sense your spirit is leading you on a journey of faith? This is likely a test or a battle. Before you act, you need to decide if you are being fired upon by the enemy or if it is friendly fire.

You Are in a War

News flash! There is a war being fought over you and your destiny. God's boot camp and tests are designed to prepare you, but to fulfill your purpose will require you to fight for your life. Boot camp teaches you how to respond when you are in a battle. An army officer friend of mine once told me, "When you are being fired upon, take cover immediately. Then take a tactical pause. Be still and do nothing. Then you can ascertain if the fire is enemy or friendly. If it is enemy fire, you give them all you got. Fire away and call for reinforcements. However, if it is friendly fire, stay put and do nothing until it is over."

"What? I'm going to be shot at by friends?" I said aloud.

This was probably the hardest lesson I have had to learn. I expected to be shot at by the "bad guys" but not by the good ones. I guess what I found even more surprising than being shot at with "friendly fire" was being betrayed by those I thought were on my team. I won't spend much time on this topic except to say that this really happened. I have experienced it, and so will you in your journey of purpose. Expect it. Train for it. Prepare for it. The army does.

Notice that you do not respond to friendly fire the way you do enemy fire. When you have determined that you are being fired upon by the good guys, take cover and do not fire back. That means keeping your mouth shut. Go underground. Wait until it stops. Do not hunt them down or murder them with your mouth. Take a tactical pause. Determine who is still loyal to you and the mission, and stay loyal to them. Regroup. Reassign positions if necessary. Then get back to work.

I wish someone would have told or taught me this lesson early in my boot camp. It was a lesson I learned much later. I learned the hard way that it is wise to be slow in letting people become members of a team or giving them pieces of your heart. As we discussed earlier, trust is built over time. *People must earn trust.* When they do, then they are given more responsibilities. This is the way the army does it. You advance through a series of well-defined job responsibilities and roles. Promotions occur when you have shown yourself to be capable and trustworthy. It would be wise to do the same. Promoting people into the inner circle of our hearts and lives should occur only as they prove trustworthy.

I let people into my heart, my life, my home, and the nonprofit I founded very easily. I am extremely naïve and trusting; thus, it is extremely upsetting to me when I am fired upon or betrayed by friends. I spend an enormous amount of time expending energy into conversations that take place only in my head instead of holding people accountable for their actions. I give grace and second chances, only to be fired upon again. My strength is my weakness. I believe in people. I am inclusive. I see potential. I invest a lot in my relationships. It is hard for me to let go and leave people to their own choices.

In one of my boot camp experiences involving friendly fire, I took a tactical pause. I felt like I had been shot in the back. As I whined about the situation, these words came to my mind: *If it is so hard for you to let people go, then be slower at letting them in.*

Somewhere in my Southern and Christian upbringing, I thought you had to let everyone into your life and inner circle. I now realize that is not necessarily true. Trusting the wrong people can lead to betrayal and friendly fire.

Fighting friendly fire with a tactical pause and silence are the best "weapons" to use. Without them, you can easily be derailed from fulfilling your destiny. To minimize these types of attacks, you need to use wisdom and seek discernment about adding people to your life and inner circle. Before giving them access to your home, your heart, your family, your finances, and the destiny you are fulfilling, you must do all you can to find out if they are trustworthy. Do background checks, talk to anyone they have worked for or with, and do not be afraid to do your "due diligence." If the individual is offended, that should be considered a "red flag." Here are three simple things to keep in mind:

Go slow.
"Hear" from your Creator.
Guard your heart.

While we cannot judge a person's heart, we can judge their "fruit." So be careful. Watch out for friendly fire. Their purpose is to stall your plans and make you quit. When you learn to use your "weapons," you will be unstoppable. Always keep in mind that "friendly fire" is a part of your boot camp to train and prepare you to fulfill your destiny. When your training is complete, you will be a fierce warrior!

Better Together

Boot camp trains you to be the best *you* you can possibly be, but it also teaches that you cannot complete your mission alone. We must depend upon others for success.

It is okay not to have all of the answers. We need to be okay with that truth. Answers can come through others, to us directly, and through the process of waiting, yes, waiting. I hate to wait. It is very hard for me. When I began to understand the details of my destiny, all I wanted to know was *how* it would happen. I spent hours and hours wondering, planning, and agonizing over the *how*. It is quite humbling to realize that I do not have all the answers I need alone. Waiting is an exercise in trust. As we pause to exhibit patience, it allows us the space to listen to others, our hearts, and our Creator for important details of our battle plan.

Relax. Take it day by day or even hour by hour if you do not have all the answers. Try to view your present circumstances through the lens of boot camp. Embrace the training that is required for water-walking, giant-slaying, history-making destinies.

There is one more benefit of boot camp—one I learned from a retired veteran. He had tears in his eyes when he shook my hand after a Sunday evening service and thanked me for the encouragement I had tried to give from the stage. I was talking about the purpose of boot camp. He told me I was right but had left out the most important thing you receive in boot camp—a battle buddy. He continued, "The guys I went through boot camp with, and the ones I continued to fight beside to execute our missions, were the closest relationships I have had in my life, outside my wife and children. When you train with someone, fight with them, and believe in a mission that is bigger than yourself, it binds you together in a way that nothing else can. Some of those men are gone now, and some I have not seen in over thirty years, but I will never forget the influence and impact they had on my life and our mission." Well said, my new friend.

A battle buddy is someone who goes through boot camp with you, holds you accountable, encourages you not to quit, and believes in the same mission you do—one you would both sacrifice your time, your talent, your treasure, and even your life for.

Without my battle buddies, I would have quit a long time ago. When you come to grips with your water-walking, giant-slaying, history-making destiny, you will be graciously surrounded by very strategic people and relationships—ones that will sustain, nourish, and support you during the difficult days of boot camp and through the dangers of war. These relationships are ones you will be grateful for all your life. They become a part of you, even if you have not seen or talked to these people for years.

In 2005, Hurricane Katrina hit the Mississippi Gulf Coast and New Orleans, Louisiana, and my heart broke. Mississippi is my home state. I was moved not only by compassion but also by a great desire for action. I immediately volunteered to go with a group from San Carlos, California, to do relief work.

When we began preparations for the trip, we were a group of strangers. By the time we returned home from our mutual experience ten days later, we were lifelong friends, bonded by an experience that is difficult to describe unless you were there to participate in it with us. It was difficult and, at the same time, immensely satisfying. Together we made a difference. Together we did more than we ever could have done alone.

The army is intentional about putting a young new recruit with other recruits who are starting out in the same place as they discover their identity before embarking on their mission. This common journey is an incredible bonding process. It is true that "we are better together." I can hear some of you asking, "Why?" There are three main reasons:

①

Big, impossible, life-changing, world-altering, incredible purposes and missions cannot be accomplished alone.

There is a "power" that multiplies whenever human beings collectively agree on anything, whether good or bad—it is the power to do the impossible!

Our team at Courage Worldwide has lived this truth firsthand. We all agree it is wrong for a child to be sold for sex. It is our common language. Because of that common belief and our core value and emphasis on unity, we believe that we can do what some would call impossible. We believe we can build a home, a Courage House, for victims of sex trafficking in every city in the world that needs one. We believe we can engage a million people to build a thousand homes in a hundred countries during the next ten years so that hundreds of thousands of children can be rescued, restored, and told the truth that they, too, were created on purpose for a purpose.

Every day, five or six days a week, for hours a day, we work toward this common goal, speaking the same language, engaged in the impossible. These individuals that I have the honor of working with at Courage Worldwide are my family, my battle buddies, and my fellow warriors. They have my back, and I have theirs. Without them, I could not do what I am created to do. Together we are able to accomplish more, faster than any of us could alone. Our collective power, energy, and creativity astound even us, but we have been brought together using our unique purposes to further an eternal purpose.

②

You have an enemy who wants you to fail at accomplishing your purpose and your mission.

Your enemy knows that if you ever realize your true identity, then your chance of success in your destiny increases. The enemy will attack you very early and frequently when you embark on a journey of purpose. Your finances, relationships, and health will all be attacked. These attacks are designed to distract you, make you forget who you are, why you are fighting, and what the mission is. You need to be reminded by other people. You will need courage, but you will also need somebody to watch your back. It is much easier to *take courage* when you are surrounded by others with weapons. Your battle buddies stand with you when you are fighting. They have resources and experiences you don't. Because they are also not emotionally involved in the battles that are personal to you, it is easier for them to encourage and support you in your situation when you just can't.

③

Small groups forge bonds that allow members to see in others what they cannot see in themselves.

We all need someone to believe in us, cheer for us, and kick us in the butt when we need it! Our battle buddies do this for us. I find it fascinating that the people I work and serve with see my potential much easier than I do. They encourage me when I get down. They pursue me when I doubt. They challenge me when I am tempted to give up, and they love me even when I fail. They help me "change the world," and your battle buddies will too.

When a group discovers that its collective identity and destiny are more powerful than the members' own individual ones, they will accomplish more than they dared to ask or imagine. They will literally change the world around them. While doing this work and pursuing the impossible, there is a bond forged that is extremely strong and rarely broken. I am so thankful for the encouragement and company of those who are called to the same mission I am. I cannot imagine doing what I do without them. They make me better.

"I will attempt something so great that it is doomed to fail unless God be in it."

—John Haggai

These words are my heart's desire. I prayed a similar prayer when I began this journey of identity and destiny.

"God, I want a story to tell that cannot be told without you in it!"

He has certainly given me that!

Ready for Your Mission

Now you are ready for your mission. You are finally ready to hear and believe what was planned for you before time began! Because of the new confidence in your identity, you will start to believe that you can accomplish the impossible: the mission assigned to you, when partnered with your Creator and your battle buddies.

Boot camp is rigorous, both physically and mentally, and is required to prepare army recruits and us for our grand purposes. It cannot be avoided, diminished, or rushed. Oh, how I wish it could! The days, months, and—yes—even years of boot camp can seem long and often uneventful, but be encouraged! You are being prepared for action; your time is coming. During this arduous preparation process, something amazing will or may have already transpired. It is difficult to detect at first. But wait for it. It is worth it, I promise.

Somewhere along the way, you'll see that the forced training and discipline become a habit instead of a chore. Our bodies, minds, and emotions begin to reflect the identity and training that has been bestowed and inflicted upon us. We see evidence of our new identity—who we were meant to be. At that point, our behaviors begin to betray our beliefs. Just like young army recruits, we begin to act out of our true identity.

I hope you understand for the first time that who you are directly correlates to *what you are to do*. Not just anyone can do what you have been assigned to do. It is your very own unique purpose.

I will end this section as we began it . . .

You were created on purpose for this purpose. Now that you know your identity, you can be released into your water-walking, giant-slaying, history-making destiny.

If you feel like you need more help in this area of finding your true identity, I created a workbook called *Uniquely You: A Faith-driven Journey to Your True Identity and Water-walking, Giant-slaying, History-making Destiny* with space to journal, questions to guide you, and encouragement for your journey. I hope it is helpful to you for your identity boot camp.

PART TWO

Stepping into Your World-changing Destiny

We must leave the human boundaries that define our lives and
step into a journey of total dependence on God's perspective
and commands; where He invades the impossible.

——Bill Johnson, *Face to Face with God*

CHAPTER 11

_____

Embracing the Impossible

*N*ow that you know *who you are*, it is time to ask, *what should I be doing?*

The answer is . . . (drumroll please) . . . *the impossible.*

That's right. You were created to do the impossible. That is why this entire journey requires courage.

When your Creator reveals the details of your destiny, your first instinct will be to scream, *"That's impossible!"* True! Alone, your destiny is impossible and requires leaving your comfort zones for the unknown.

All of the thought and planning that went into creating you was not so you could cruise through life sleeping on high thread count sheets and eating bonbons. You were created for great exploits! You were created to change the world. However, a transition must first take place. You have to embrace the impossible.

Venturing into the Unknown

As you daily embrace your identity as a child of God, you can be confident that your Creator will lead you in the path He has chosen for you. You were created to walk on water, slay giants with pebbles, and change the course of history. But you will not get there by being comfortable or playing it safe. Water-walking, giant-slaying, history-making destinies are found squarely in the unknown. There is rarely a strategic plan or well-marked road map to get there. Sadly, few have dared to venture on this journey of faith. The destination is unfamiliar, and the voyage is extremely uncomfortable—especially in the beginning.

Still, you have to go. And now that you know who you really are, I am certain you are restless to do something, the *something* only you can do. Navigating from the known to the unknown, from the boat to the water, from the possible to the impossible, is the only way. It is challenging, awkward, and even a little dangerous. However, before you can receive the details of your destiny, you must learn to get comfortable with being uncomfortable. You must get out of your proverbial boat.

Have you ever tried to get out of a boat when it is sitting on the water? There is simply no graceful way to do it. *Picture it with me:* You have one foot on the relatively solid surface of the boat while at the same time, you are looking for another fixed surface (like a dock) to place your other foot.

An exchange must take place before you can lift your body out of the boat. Of course, the boat will not be still. Your body and the boat are in constant motion as the boat pitches back and forth in the water. You feel unstable and lack confidence in your ability to make the transition at all, much less make it gracefully. You long for a hand to hold. The entire process is precarious.

Now imagine this transition from the boat to walking on the water. "Impossible!" our minds scream. When we hear that word, we remain where we are—comfortable, yet longing and restless for more.

I like my comfort zones. I worked hard for them. I wrestle with the idea of the unknown. No one likes being tossed to and fro by waves of uncertainty. I like to feel confident, doing things I know how to do and doing them well. When things are good, I want them to stay that way forever. Of course, this has not been my life experience. Over time, we all learn that nothing stays the same. Change is inevitable. And it is also necessary. Why? Because change transitions us from our comfort zones to the unknown and is often the impetus our Creator uses to move us from where we are to where He wants us to be.

There is only one reason I am a willing participant in the transition process: *I want to change the world.*

I do have to admit I would really like a detailed, strategic plan listing tangible steps to my destiny along with an implementation timeline. Instead, I sense a whisper, a divine invitation to leave all I know. I am scared to death but also reassured by my Creator that I can face and overcome my fears, my "what ifs," and insecurities one step at a time. My deepest desire to be and do everything for which I am created stirs and churns within me. My heart aches to do the impossible, even if it means leaving the place I love.

I Choose to Believe

One of my most challenging transitions began on an ordinary day. I sat reading my Bible in my flower garden, my dog Jake sleeping at my feet. As I read the ancient text, I sensed the approach of change. I had been extremely comfortable for a long time, but on that day, trouble brewed in my paradise. I was searching for answers to a problem that was too big for me to solve. The story I read of Abram and his nephew Lot mirrored my own. They were experiencing *strife*.

Strife? That was it! That was what I was feeling. My husband, Michael, and I were experiencing intense strife. We own an energy consulting business, which is much like riding a roller coaster with no seat belt. Natural gas prices fluctuate minute by minute. One day you can be riding waves of profit, and the next, drowning in a sea of debt. We were experiencing the latter. We owed more money than we had in our bank account, and it was due *now*. That qualifies as strife, I think. It was extremely uncomfortable and terrifying. And it was the very thing my Creator would use to transition us from where we were to where we were supposed to be.

We had tried everything we could think of to keep from drowning in the debt we faced. This financial crisis threatened to swallow us and everything we had worked so hard for. We cashed in our 401(k)s and our kids' college funds. We sought out a bankruptcy attorney who told us bankruptcy would not provide cover or protection for our unique situation. Friends graciously loaned and gifted us money, which was a very humbling experience. Did I mention that I was way out of my comfort zone and how impossible it all seemed?

The unknown loomed. I had no idea what to do. I prayed for courage. I embraced my identity as a child of God, believing the impossible would become possible.

During this season, I wrote a personal vow inspired by page 2,035 in my Bible. *Against all hope, and in spite of my circumstances, I will choose to believe. I will not waver with unbelief because I know my Creator has the power to do what is promised even in the midst of the unknown.* There on the same page, I had written myself a note during a previous time of struggle with change and transition:

When we believe, an exchange takes place in heaven, and our situation is about to change—hold on!

I was holding on tight.

Strife and fear are not good. They are paralyzing. *What should I do, God?* Courage is action in spite of fear, so what action should I take to propel me out of this mess into my destiny?

Sell your house.

What?

Sell my house? Confusion flooded my thoughts. Although our financial situation was bleak, I had childlike faith that it would change. I loved my life, my home. Even though we were going through strife, I did not want to leave. I was a room mom at my kids' school. Both my husband and I worked from home. I was on staff at our church. I had started a nonprofit organization with some friends called Courage to Be You, Inc., to help people find their purpose. I had conquered my fear of public speaking and was shouting the life-changing message from a stage and to anyone who would listen that they were created on purpose for a purpose. I thought I was finally doing all I was created for, and for the first time in my life, I felt fully alive.

To make things even sweeter, I loved my husband, Michael, more than I had on the day I married him, and I was confident he loved me just as much. My little boys were doing well in school, and my oldest son had become a fine young man of whom I was so very proud. We had amazing friends that felt more like family.

Leaving was not on my radar. Leaving was not my plan. I did not want to transition to another place.

However, the financial storm had hit. Waves of debt crashed over us while the strife weighed us down. Though my faith was strong, I was terrified of going bankrupt or being sued by our clients. The waves were so high. I was sure we would drown. But in the midst of the tempest, a hand was offered to steady my boat. Change loomed. Transition beckoned. An invitation was offered. It just was not what I planned or wanted at the time.

Sell my house? My home? Go where? This was my divine invitation. I had much to ponder and process.

After much thought and prayer, I knew the answer. We had to step out in faith—sell our home, take the equity to save our business, and move somewhere yet to be disclosed. Still, I struggled to say yes. I loved my home, my neighborhood, and the life we had built there. Michael and I had moved from Mississippi to the San Francisco Bay Area the day after we married. We lived there for fourteen years; eight of those years were spent in the house we were now asked to give up. *My home.* The known for the unknown.

Memories flooded my thoughts as I entertained a move. Small, intimate family Christmases, loud Thanksgivings, supper clubs, late-night tuck-ins and early morning snuggles, birthday parties, girlfriend groups, bouncy houses, waiting up late for teenagers, sending children off to first grade and college then welcoming them home again. Our friends had become our California family. There had been so much love and laughter in that place. I believed I would grow old there, loving my husband long after the kids had gone, waiting to greet grandbabies.

Yet I believed we had received a divine invitation to sell our home and pack up everything we owned with no idea where we would go. Was I losing my mind?

As I contemplated the unknown, I was reminded how very restless I had become in my very comfortable life—before the strife. The things I once had a passion for had become routine and mundane. I sensed a new dream, one bigger than I could imagine, was about to be birthed. Writing a book, speaking to thousands, traveling the world, opening homes for people who needed them—it all seemed and sounded so impossible, especially in light of my circumstances. But I believed it all. I just assumed I would be doing all of it from my home in the San Francisco Bay Area, but change was coming. I did not think it would be as drastic as a new address.

I wept as I contemplated the dream that was revealed to me. I wanted it all. I had many questions, but I also had my answer.

Yes, we would go.

But what would Michael say? Would he think I was crazy? Probably. One evening, I explained to him the dream that had captured my heart. Let's just say he did not see it as a divine invitation, and he certainly did not embrace the idea of selling our home without knowing where we were going. Though I could understand his reluctance, I was confused. I truly believed this was what we were supposed to do, but my husband could not see it. For two weeks, I fretted and prayed. Then one morning, Michael said, "Okay, let's do it."

I was strangely excited. I hired a realtor and quickly put the house up for sale, even though we still had no idea where we were going. Our friends and family thought we were scared, crazy, or just running from our problems. They were wrong. We were preparing to walk on water. I wanted to do it well. I wanted the transition to be grace-filled.

Our house sold in just one week—at the height of the market, before the housing collapse in 2007. We had thirty days to pack, move, enroll our kids in school, and start our new life. We still had no idea where we were going, but I was confident this transition would lead to my destiny.

And it did!

CHAPTER 12

Responding to Divine Invitations

*A*ny major transition leading you to your water-walking, giant-slaying, history-making destiny will start with a divine invitation sent directly to your heart from your Creator. However, the challenge is to determine whether the invitation is truly divine or if it is simply a desperate human attempt to fulfill your own dreams or solve your own problems.

In my experience, a divine invitation is much crazier and riskier than anything I can come up with on my own. My dreams, ideas, and solutions tend to be logical. They have a safety net or savings account attached to them and are very much something I can do within my own power and personality.

If the invitation is indeed divine, it will scare you to death. It will seem impossible.

Initially, you will feel as if you cannot do it, while at the same time, you will long to try. Over time, as the idea settles deep within you, you will *want* to do it. You will then dare to believe you *can* do it. The invitation will feel so right, yet you will be reluctant to leave all you know.

Waiting for a divine invitation is a must. I did it wrong for so long. I did it my way. I happen to be a very capable person. I am a problem solver, and I make decisions quickly and confidently. But when faced with situations beyond my control and much bigger than my resources, I tend to become paralyzed. That is what fear does to you—it stops you dead in your tracks. It is hard to even think or pray. After paralyzing fear comes reactive panic. Panic makes you feel you must do something—anything—even if it is the wrong thing. You believe doing something is better than doing nothing. Your response becomes a frantic reaction. It rarely proves wise. Been there, done that.

I had lived the first forty years of my life reacting to whatever life threw my way, taking matters into my own hands without consulting my Creator, and coming up with my own desperate solutions. That is not a recipe for a successful water-walking destiny. There is a better way.

When you sense a divine invitation from your Creator to leave your comfort zone for the unknown, when you sense change or transition is coming, you have to ask the hard questions, process your feelings and fears, and then seek the advice of other people experienced in grace-filled transitions. After you have done that, take all of your thoughts, observations, feelings, questions, and doubts and write them down in a journal, unedited. This will help you untangle your feelings from the facts. It will help you discern if you are sensing a truly divine invitation from your Maker.

If it is, do not hesitate. Get out of the boat. Jump in!

While there certainly is a time to pause and ponder, I have found that divine invitations do not last forever. I do not want to miss the boat or, worse, have my boat tipped over and be thrown head-first into the deep end. Though I may be scared to death of leaving my comfort zones, I am more afraid of missing what I am designed to be, see, and do. I want to experience it all. Don't you?

To make sure I don't miss divine opportunities, I intentionally study successful water walkers and their transitions from the known to the unknown. One of my favorite studies is the life of Peter, a fisherman turned fisher of men and the original water walker. How I would love to interview him and ask him these questions:

Why were you the only one to get out of the boat, a place you were safe and comfortable?

How did you conquer your fear?

Where did you find the courage?

Would you do it again?

What was going through your mind?

Did anyone encourage you to do it?

These questions could be asked of anyone pursuing their world-changing destiny. However, in my life, I could not find many flesh-and-blood people doing just that. Peter inspired me. An ordinary man who craved the impossible. He seemed to wrestle with the tension of wanting to be safe but wanting to walk on water. It seemed he knew the secret; without a divine invitation, he would have literally drowned.

Before you jump headfirst into the waves of the unknown, pause long enough to confirm there is a divine invitation. Start with a long, honest prayer between you and your Creator. Talk with other water walkers you know, and if you cannot find many in your own life, then study the pages of the Bible or other biographies of those who dared to leave the known for the unknown. Journal your thoughts. While a divine invitation will give rise to fear, you will also feel a rightness and excitement that gives you the courage to move out of your boat of comfort and begin considering the impossible possible.

Grab Hold of Healthy Fear

Accepting a divine invitation requires that we fear God. When I was young, I thought that fearing God meant I was supposed to be afraid of Him, but I never was. My view of God was largely shaped by my dad, who loved me madly. I assumed God did too. My dad was a strict and consistent disciplinarian but only punished me when I deserved it, like when I was being blatantly disobedient. It seemed to my little girl's mind that God followed the same pattern as my dad— loving me madly and disciplining me as warranted by my actions. Thus I tried very hard to be a good girl. I was scared to death to get in trouble and hated disappointing anyone.

My dad loves to tell the story of my one and only spanking. I was five years old, and my brother and I had been talking during "big" church. I always had a hard time sitting still and being quiet. Even now, whispering is still difficult for me to curtail. My dad leaned over during the service and gave us *the look*. We knew he meant business, yet we continued to talk, giggle, and squirm. Not long afterward, we were promised a spanking when we got home.

When we arrived home, we ate lunch, and my dad started watching Sunday afternoon football. I thought he had forgotten all about our promised discipline. At halftime, we were called, one at a time, into the bathroom—that is where Dad held his private disciplinary conversations with his children. I courageously volunteered to go first because I was the oldest and wanted to protect my siblings. As soon as the door closed, I started screaming and crying. My dad said, with amusement in his voice, "Sister, I haven't even spanked you yet." Then I got the "it's going to hurt me more than it is going to hurt you" speech. I feared my dad, but I was not afraid of him. I respected him. After my promised punishment, my dad said something that has remained with me to this day: "I have to discipline you to teach you. I told you that you would be punished, and now I have to keep my word. I want you to depend upon my word just like you do my love."

I believe our Creator wants us to know the same thing. We may not like the discipline that comes into our lives via boot camp, as I referred to earlier, but in times of transition from the known to the unknown, we need to know that our Creator can be depended upon. In my journal, I recorded a quote someone once sent to me.

> *To fear the Lord is to recognize God for who He is and who He says He is. Holy, almighty, righteous, pure, all-knowing, all-powerful, all-wise, and in control of this crazy planet. When we regard our Creator correctly, we regard ourselves correctly. When we recognize who our Creator is, then we recognize our place in His plans. We then fall at His feet in humble respect and only then will He show us the way—the way chosen for us.*

We need a big God. We need to understand who our Creator is. How does this happen? For me, it is very often in creation. That is where God really shows off. It is where He communicates to me that He is all I will ever need and that He alone is big enough to carry me through all of my life's transitions.

When my circumstances seem scary and overwhelming, which I feel when change is coming, I go for a hike. When my problems threaten to engulf me, or I feel my Creator is leading me to do the impossible, I immerse myself in creation. I need to feel small. I need wide-open spaces.

During the time before our move, one of my favorite places to hike was high atop a cliff called Devil's Slide, located on Highway 1. One shoulder of the highway is the Pacific Ocean and the other is the face of a cliff. It is a treacherous, beautiful drive. Devil's Slide is a vista point with a trailhead that leads up to a higher lookout. I would climb that hill, watching the highway and the cars become smaller and smaller.

As I climbed, I became aware of the smell and sound of the ocean. That part of the Pacific coast is wild, untamed, and fierce. The waves roar and slam violently against the rock walls. I stood with my feet on the edge of the cliff, staring out into the vast ocean. In that moment, I felt like I was the only person on the planet. The thundering waves pounded at my soul. The wind whipped at a frenzied pace. I stood as still as I could and felt the power of creation and the power of my Creator. I was in awe. My world and my struggles instantly seemed inconsequential. The impossible became possible.

I have also been awed at the *bigness* of my Creator at the top of Half Dome in Yosemite National Park. I have only had the courage to make it up the infamous cables twice. It is a grueling all-day hike, topped off with a harrowing climb up a slick granite rock face holding onto cables with your hands—praying you do not slip and fall into the abyss. The effort is worth it. When you stand on the top edge of that enormous slab of granite, the expansive green valley below seems to disappear under the massive rock. Looking down and focusing my attention on the valley floor, I can barely make out the movement below. Cars look like Hot Wheels in a tiny toy village.

The top of Half Dome is the size of a football field. I search out a crevice where I can be alone. There it happens again—I begin to feel small. As my own stature changes, everything else in my world begins to get smaller too. As I shrink, I feel my Creator's majesty in the mountains. I feel my Creator's peace in the green pastures and His presence in the vista. I welcome it all. I do not have to have all the answers. I do not have to know the future because my Creator does.

Knowing I am small and my Creator is big helps me face His divine invitations. And when transition looms, I may be uncertain of what I will need or the right path to take, but God knows. All the insurmountable obstacles my brain imagines are no match for His love for me. When I consider the force of the ocean or the majesty of the mountains, the challenges in my life that seem so daunting now appear insignificant. I receive the confidence that my Creator is big enough to handle anything I encounter on this planet. Fearing Him makes it all possible.

I need a big God if I am ever going to leave the known for the unknown. At that particular time in my life, it involved an unplanned move and an enormous debt.

Take Time to Look Back

Looking back gives us perspective on previous life transitions and prepares us for more in the future. Often when we are in the middle of change or transition, it is hard to see what purpose the event serves in moving us toward our destinies. Often, we gain a fresh understanding only after the transition is complete. Trying to figure it all out while in the middle of it can prove frustrating and confusing. However, when we begin to settle into a new comfort zone, we can review the transition, looking for the "a-ha" moments of how we were being moved further into our water-walking, giant-slaying, history-making destinies.

Transitions are not random acts of fate but events orchestrated uniquely by our Creator to prepare and propel us into our unique purpose. Without them, we would never go. I would have never left the Bay Area without the financial storm. That storm created the perfect situation for my inaugural water walking.

Peter, our fisherman turned water walker, also encountered a storm the night he walked on water. I wonder if he contemplated his transition many years after the fact. He was a capable fisherman quite comfortable in a boat out on the open sea. However, on his own, he knew he could not get out of that boat and walk on water. No matter how capable we may think we are, belief in ourselves alone is not sufficient to change the world. Our Creator must orchestrate transitions tailored specifically for us.

Have you reviewed your transitions? Looking back, can you see past your fear and consider if His divine hand was moving you from the known to the unknown? Was a storm required to move you from where you were to where you were supposed to be?

Our knee-jerk reaction to difficult situations, divine or not, is to hunker down at the bottom of the boat, quaking in fear. But if we can look at transitions as divinely orchestrated methods to get us to move from where we are to where we are supposed to be, it can help us gain confidence in the process. Remembering the past helps us see how we are constantly being prepared for our future. Looking back is a secret that helps transition us to the journey ahead.

Just Let Go!

You have a divine invitation and a healthy fear of your Creator, and you are now seeing how your circumstances have been uniquely orchestrated to transition you from where you are to where you are supposed to be—but wait! The journey to your water-walking, giant-slaying, history-making destiny requires that you must leave some things behind.

Before you throw your leg over the side, there is something very important that must happen first. You have to loosen your grip on all that you think is yours, on all that you hold dear, on all that keeps you safe and comfortable. You have to let go.

Accepting a divine invitation is impossible when you hold tightly to something or someone. It does not matter whom or what you hold onto—ideas, relationships, homes, jobs, or thought patterns. Clutching anything or anyone too tightly is a recipe for disaster. You have to let go. If you do not, whatever "it" is might be pried from your hands—and trust me, that is not fun.

Repeat after me: "Just let go!"

A friend once asked if I had ever had my heart broken. I said no. However, the question stayed with me for a few days, tugging at my memories. It shocked me when I realized my heart had been broken twice by the same person, my eldest son. It was not intentional on his part. The only reason he had the power to break my heart was because of the death grip I had on him. For his sake and mine, he was pried out of my hands. Twice.

The first time it happened, I did not learn my lesson very well. I just regripped him and held on tighter. The second time was as painful as the first, but I finally learned a truth that startled me even more than the pain, one that ultimately allowed me to let go: *my Creator loves my son more than I do.*

By letting go, I learned that there was a unique plan for my son's life that was bigger and grander than anything I had ever imagined. My son's choices were his own. From then on, I got the pure pleasure of just loving him for who he is. By letting him go, he was free to become the person he was created to be. I learned that by holding onto him so tightly, I had stopped him from growing into that man.

I also had to learn this secret with regard to "things." I had to practice loosening my grip daily on the things I thought were mine. Every paycheck was an opportunity to give to others, not just meet my own needs. Giving helped loosen my grip. Every time I pulled up in my driveway, I practiced releasing my house, thankful for the privilege of its use but reminding myself that I must be willing to give it up if I wanted to fulfill my destiny.

When I heard the still, small voice from within me whisper, *"Sell the house,"* I was able to say yes only because I had practiced releasing it daily. Of course, I was sad—I'm not superhuman—but I was not devastated or distraught. Letting go of something meant it was time for a new transition.

When my husband and I let go of our 401(k) and the kids' college funds—all to reduce the business losses—I remember crying, "This is our savings, our family's security for the future!" Then I felt a whisper I attributed to my Creator, saying He would be my security and my savings account. As His child, I could trust in His love for me and my family. God's plan often flies in the face of man's logic.

Other times I have had to let go of a career, a position I loved, as well as relationships that were important to me. It was difficult, but in time I saw that letting go was divinely orchestrated to move me further into my destiny.

Letting go of people and things loosens our grip and allows us to transition from the known to the unknown gracefully. When we give, we can expect to receive. What are you holding on to tightly that may be keeping you from your world-changing destiny? Loosen your grip and see what happens. Your destiny is worth it.

Two days after our house sold, I went to church and started telling people we were moving. Over and over, our friends asked, "Where?"

"I don't know," I answered. At first, I felt ridiculous uttering those words, but then I remembered the lessons I learned in boot camp and during other transitions. *I do not know* is a perfectly acceptable answer! My Creator does. That lessens my stress. I remembered that my Creator promised to lead me on the path He had chosen for me. It was not my responsibility; my family and I would be shown a path that aligned with our destiny.

During one of these conversations, a friend of mine said, "I have a rental house in Sacramento. My tenants gave their notice last night. Want to move to Sacramento?" Sacramento. I had never been to Sacramento. I did not know a soul in Sacramento. Was this a divine invitation?

I asked my husband. "Whatever," he answered. Then I asked my Creator. "Yes," was the divine answer I sensed. We immediately let go of all we held dear and headed east to Sacramento. I was confident my destiny was there—even though it was a very difficult time for our family. Time proved the move was divine. Since land is much cheaper in the Sacramento area than in the San Francisco Bay Area, we purchased a fifty-acre ranch within four years. We opened the first Courage House for girls rescued from sex trafficking while opening another home in Tanzania, Africa. There is no question in my mind that the invitation was divine. But even when we know the invitation is divine, it can still be hard.

Expect Obstacles

No one promised water-walking, giant-slaying, history-making destinies would be easy. If this destiny thing were easy, everyone would be doing it! Pursuing a life of purpose requires a fierce determination not to quit in the face of adversity. To transition from the known to the unknown, you will need some teeth-gritting, nose-to-the-grindstone, *divinely-bestowed tenacity!* However, it must be coupled with an awareness of a purpose that is greater than the immediate circumstances. I tried to do that as we unpacked in our new rental home, but it was hard.

We tend to quit if we do not see there is a purpose—something bigger than ourselves—in the midst of our difficult circumstances, insurmountable obstacles, and painful experiences. We grow weary and lose heart when we do not understand the "why." Earlier, I told you that others are waiting for you to have the courage to be and do all that you were created to. It matters if you are being you. It matters to someone if you quit. Your destiny is designed to meet the needs of others. Use this thought to motivate you through whatever storm you are facing.

We are considered blessed when we persevere.

James 5:11, paraphrase mine

I laughed when I first read that. I think someone sent it to me as encouragement. However, I do not *feel* very blessed when I am in the midst of teeth-gritting, painful persevering. I *feel* anything but blessed. However, we learned in boot camp that our feelings are not necessarily the truth. We must *choose* to believe it matters that we persevere. It matters that we overcome, for there is a purpose—something bigger that we cannot see. Pain and suffering will eventually lead to a blessing if we do not quit.

The fulfillment of our destinies depends upon us not quitting. I have this fear that I am going to miss what is planned for me. That is why I do not give up. It is why I have resolved not to quit. I believe there is a great harvest coming if I do not become weary of doing good. When I do not see results or when my circumstances are not changing as fast as I think they should, this vow is my motivation. I believe that my efforts, my prayers, and my suffering will not be in vain. I see purpose in my efforts even when I do not immediately see the outcome I desire. The promise of my destiny tells me to work hard, not give up, and that in time, I will walk on water. I must persevere. But I still hate that word. My default mode likes easy, but I know I was designed for so much more. You are, too. Take courage. Do not quit.

I was raised by parents who grew up on farms, so I love analogies about growing things. I learned that for crops to grow, the soil has to be prepared, the seeds planted, and the ground watered—all by the farmer. To ensure a good harvest, the farmer must be vigilant about protecting his garden from weeds and pests. This is a picture of perseverance, of working for that which is unseen.

As any farmer will tell you, there is a tremendous investment of time, energy, and money spent before the first green sprouts in a garden ever appear. The farmer participates in this backbreaking process because he is confident his efforts will result in a harvest. He perseveres for a purpose. He works with the harvest in mind. He knows his efforts matter.

So can we.

We can have the same confidence that our work, our waiting, and our sometimes difficult circumstances are all a part of the plan to transition us from the known to the unknown, the place where we will find our purpose. We must participate in the process of realizing our destinies.

Most of us loathe the word *perseverance* because the implication is that it is going to require hard work and commitment. We like fast and easy. Perseverance is neither. Nor does it feel good or natural. But then again, neither does walking on water or transitioning into the unknown. However, it is exactly what we were created to do. Instead of fighting against it or, worse, quitting, we must *choose to participate in the process*. Our Creator knows us—what we value and hold onto—and He uniquely orchestrates circumstances that require our perseverance for the privilege of participating in His divine purposes and plans for this world. Which will a teenager appreciate more—a car given to him by his parents or one he buys after saving for years? Which will he take better care of and be more responsible for? The car he had to work for, of course. We all know it is true. It is human nature.

That truth makes me want to try harder and run faster, and, most importantly, it keeps me from quitting when I cannot see immediate results. None of us felt excitement when our moving van pulled into the driveway of our new home in Sacramento, but I was confident we were transitioning into our destiny. I consciously decided to actively participate in the process. I chose to do what I could do. I slapped a smile on my face, unpacked our boxes, and made our new house a home for our family. I chose to believe in my destiny and not give up in spite of my feelings. I took control of my negative thoughts, which ultimately changed the way I felt and acted. My efforts affected others.

Little by little, our family and business grew stronger, and the dream laid on my heart in the Bay Area became real in Sacramento. It would not have happened without this difficult transition. On Christmas morning, months after the move, I woke up and sensed a silent whisper:

> *You did not lose your home and have to move because of financial ruin. Your financial situation was the impetus, the uniquely orchestrated circumstances I used to get you to the place where I will birth the dream I placed on your heart. You did not do anything wrong. I moved you. You needed a new address to fulfill your destiny. You would have never moved without the financial situation.*

Peace flooded my soul. Those words gave me courage.

Take Courage

Are you going through a difficult transition or unwanted change? I pray my story gives you encouragement. Changes are scary because they require that we leave a place we know and travel to one we do not. They leave us feeling inept and unsure. They paralyze us, making it feel impossible to advance. Those feelings are not truth. You can do this—one step at a time, one day at a time. There is a plan and purpose for your life. The blessings will come if you choose to persevere and participate in the process. Will you? Resolve right now to take every negative thought and feeling captive so you can move forward to fulfill your purpose on this planet. Take courage.

Courage is simply action in the face of fear.

It is not a feeling or a personality trait; it is an intentional choice—something you *do*, not something you *feel*. This was a revelation to me, and I learned another secret to successful, grace-filled transitions: You must *take* courage, an action.

I hope that by now you are encouraged to embrace the transition or change you are facing right now. I wrote this chapter hoping you would begin to see transition and change in a different light, realizing that your destiny lies outside your comfort zones in the middle of the unknown.

When a divine invitation has been issued, you will be taught many lessons as your Creator orchestrates unique circumstances to transition you from where you are to where you are meant to be. You must choose to persevere and participate in the process because something is going on that is much bigger than you. You will be required to loosen your grip on the things and people you love. Courage will be required as you walk through the invisible wall of fear that is keeping you from moving forward.

I mentioned earlier the idea of having a battle buddy, a must-have for birthing and fulfilling your dreams. You absolutely need *intimate, authentic relationships*. Not just any relationships but relationships with others who have left their comfort zones, given up all they held dear, and transitioned into their world-changing destinies.

People who try to do big things often feel alone in spite of our Creator's intangible presence and still, small whisper. Often, we need the tangible company of another person a few steps ahead of us, fighting for his or her destiny too. Sometimes we all need a word of encouragement or a swift kick in the butt to get us moving. Sometimes I need the encouragement of someone who has walked through his or her own invisible wall of fear and experienced God's grace in their life. I need someone to believe in me. I need my battle buddy. They give me the courage to move forward.

When I sense a divine invitation into the unknown, the only people I want to talk to or want praying for me are other experienced water walkers. I do not find them very often in my comfort zones. The other people who surround you in your boat of comfort are usually not water walkers either. The non–water walkers in your life will try to hang onto your leg so you cannot be and do all God has called you to do. They will call you crazy. Once you start trying to get out of your boat, you will stir some things up for them. You will rattle their cage of comfort. You will rock the boat, and most people do not like that. They like the status quo. They like you in their comfort zone.

My advice? Do not look back. If they hang on your leg, shake them off and keep on going. Do not let anyone hold you back. Do not let anyone speak negativity into your life or tell you that you cannot do what your destiny calls you to do. Do not listen to them. *You get to choose who will speak into your life.*

Find some water walkers and hang out with them. You might get a little wet, but it is better than never having the courage to be you. Ask questions about how they found the courage to get out of their boat. Find people who have persevered through difficult circumstances, courageously believing in God for their harvest. Have them pray for you. Have them speak truth to you. Read your Bible or other books of faith, and read biographies of water walkers, giant slayers, and history makers and do what they did.

Be courageous. *Do something.*

CHAPTER 13

The Courage to Seem Crazy

*"Let us build here a church so great that those who come
after us will think us mad ever to have attempted it."*

—etched above a cathedral in Seville, Spain

*A*s we were settling into our new life, Michael joined me and Jake on our
morning walks. We walked and talked, enjoying a new level of intimacy
birthed in our marriage. One morning, I realized I had never told Michael about
the dream-filled destiny within my heart. However, the thought of doing so
scared me to death. I did not want my husband to think I was crazy, or worse—
religious. It would take an enormous amount of courage for me to tell my husband
the extent of those dreams.

With courage, I concocted a plan. I took my husband out for dinner, ordered
a fabulous bottle of wine, and shared the dreams I secretly carried. Nervously I
began to speak, pouring out my heart and all the dreams that had been locked
away for so long—an international nonprofit organization, speaking engage-
ments around the world, a book, homes called Courage Houses, and income
generators that included an exclusive merchandise line and Courage Cafés. I was

talking ninety miles an hour. Through it all, my husband did not say a word. I never gave him a chance. His face never once betrayed his thoughts. As I laid out my dreams, I began to *feel* foolish.

In light of our financial circumstances, these dreams made no sense. As I spoke them aloud for the first time, they sounded crazy, even to me. However, I believed them all. When I finished, I took a deep breath and poured another glass of wine, waiting for my husband to speak. When he did, I almost fell off my chair.

> *"The only thing stopping you is the anchor you*
> *have placed around your own neck."*

I caught my breath as I grasped the fact that my husband believed in me more than I believed in myself. Revelation dawned. My fear had been self-imposed! My feelings were not truth! What if I had listened to the voices of doubt and kept silent? Without courage, I would have never heard his words or experienced the elation I felt at that moment.

I remembered what I learned about courage: *action in the face of fear*. Not a feeling or a personality trait, but an intentional choice—something you *do*, not something you *feel*. I had shown courage by being vulnerable in sharing my dreams with Michael. I took a risk that he would reject them, or worse, me! I had walked through the invisible wall of fear. Confidence surged within me. My husband's belief fueled the dreams in my heart and gave me the courage to take steps toward making them a reality. Yes, I was still scared. My dreams were huge and seemed impossible. I felt paralyzed by the sheer weight of them, but I declared fear would never rob me of anything ever again—especially my destiny. That night, while talking with my husband, I realized that courage simply meant moving forward one step at a time, even when I felt afraid. Courage is a choice, not a feeling.

It was the same for Ordinary, a character in Bruce Wilkinson's book *The Dream Giver*.

> With every step back toward the middle of Familiar, Ordinary grew more comfortable. But he quickly noticed he was also growing sad again. And he knew why; with each step he took, he was leaving his Big Dream farther behind. Then he heard the Dream Giver again.
>
> "Why are you going back?" he asked.
>
> Ordinary stopped. "Because I'm afraid! Leaving Familiar feels too scary and too risky."

"Yes, it does."

"But if I was supposed to do this Big Dream," Ordinary exclaimed, "then I'm sure I wouldn't feel so afraid!"

"Yes, you would," said the Dream Giver. "Every Nobody does."

Ordinary hung his head. He thought for a moment. "But you could take away the fear. Please take the fear away!" he begged. "If you don't, I can't go on!"

"Yes, you can," the Dream Giver said. "Take courage, Ordinary."

And then he was gone. Ordinary saw his choice clearly now. He could either keep his comfort or his Dream.[10]

Which will you choose?

We all get scared and long for comfort and security. Daily we must ask for the courage to move outside our comfort zones through the invisible wall of fear. Fear cheats us, attempting to stop us from proceeding into our history-making futures. Fear entices us to settle for mediocrity. It makes us afraid to cast off the anchor we have hung around our necks. It makes us believe we are less than we are.

Do you have the courage to be you—the *you* that you were created to be? Prove it. Set a goal. Speak your dream aloud. Tell someone you are going to do what scares you. Take intentional steps toward your dream, regardless of your circumstances and in spite of your fear. That is courage. Come on, get out of that boat!

There was a point six months after we moved when I was very discouraged. The dreams I carried inside of me still lay dormant, hidden away with no visible means of ever happening. One night during this time, I had a nighttime dream. This dream proved "divine" to me in gaining a new perspective about my circumstances. In my dream, we were moving to a new city. My entire family was squished into a moving van, along with all of our belongings. We pulled into the driveway of the house we bought. It was small, old, and dark, located right under a freeway. The front yard was a sidewalk. I walked inside and saw there was not a window in the entire place. It was ugly and smelled of mold and mildew. The noise from the freeway was deafening. It sounded like the cars and trucks were driving right through the house. I *hated* this place. I could not believe we had bought it. I began to lug boxes into the house, feeling so alone. There was heavy darkness all around me, and I kept thinking, *I am stuck here—nothing will ever change.* This was not what I had hoped for. I continued to drag in boxes from the truck. After a while, I filled the little house with boxes, but the truck was still half full of our stuff. The rest of our things would not fit. I was miserable.

Then I woke up.

For days, the dream haunted me, and heaviness wrapped around me like a blanket. I could not shake the feelings of doom and gloom. I usually do not have dreams, much less remember them so vividly. I am not prone to visions, and I do not usually walk around with heaviness and darkness surrounding me. When I finally consulted my Creator, I sensed these words:

The dreams you carry were placed there by Me and will not fit into your present circumstances, so do not even try. Do not trust what you see, trust Me. I will birth what I have planted within you when the time is right.

The heaviness lifted. I was encouraged, and I held onto my dreams.

Time proved my feelings were not telling me the truth about my situation. In March 2007, I sensed it was time—time to move forward into my destiny, including conferences, books, homes, and for "more than I could dare ask or imagine." You have to understand, nothing had changed in our circumstances. We were still living in my friend's rental house, not knowing a single soul, still struggling financially, and at the same time, one of my sons was being bullied at school. However, right in the middle of all that mess, I felt the whisper of my Creator, the issue of a divine invitation. And I freaked out.

I am not ready! I do not have anything to say! I have too much to say! I am scared! I have not spoken on a stage in two years! Who will listen? Everyone will think I am crazy. I do not have time. I do not have any money. Two of my kids are still at home. They need me! I do not know anyone in this town. How do I plan and market something without knowing a living, breathing soul in this town? Who will live in these homes, these Courage Houses? How will I pay for them? What if no one comes? What if no one wants to read my book?

The words poured from my mouth, revealing what was in my heart—the false beliefs I had claimed in the months since our move from the Bay Area. I had come to believe and own the fact that I was responsible for all the results. Oops. Paralyzing fears, clamoring doubts, and glaring inadequacies rushed forward unrestrained. I truly could not imagine how I would do what was asked of me. It all seemed so impossible. The answer was simple: *Alone, I could not.* Running outside to the wide-open spaces, hiking a mountain to feel small, and listening for the still, small voice of my Creator, I took my thoughts and feelings captive. I listened again for the divine invitation to come out onto the water. However, this time I reminded myself that I was not responsible for the results. My job was to participate in the process. I had a funny feeling that the steps of faith I was about to take were going to make me look a little crazy. Thank heaven my husband believed in me.

Up until that time, I had closely guarded all the dreams I carried in my heart. My husband was the one person I had shared everything with. I pondered why. Fear. Fear of looking crazy. Fear that no one would believe me. Fear that I would not have the answers when they asked me how I was going to pull it all off, so I remained silent. Now I knew my Creator wanted me to tell everyone, and I mean *everyone*, all the dreams hidden inside of me. This was my act of courage, my leap of faith.

Courage Houses; Courage Cafés; Courage Conferences; Courage Consulting, Counseling, and Coaching; international travel; and speaking. Though I believed it all, I was not sure anyone else would. It seemed the dreams deposited within me and the ways they would happen would only come to fruition if I began to speak them aloud. I needed to "go out on a limb." But what if I couldn't do it? What if people laughed? What if I was crazy and had made it all up?

What if? What if? What if?

I had a choice. I could remain silent, being more concerned for my reputation than the fulfillment of my destiny, or I could speak aloud all I believed and see if the mountains moved and the divine happened.

I chose to speak.

In that simple act of faith, the simple yet crazy and scary act of speaking, I came to believe in the fullness of my destiny. My voice was the vehicle of birth.

I wrote down everything that I believed. I called it a business plan, but it was more of a vision statement. It felt like I was taking shorthand from heaven. And then the inevitable happened.

When I got the courage to speak it all aloud to anyone who would listen, exactly what I feared happened. People told me I was crazy. People told me I could never do what I believed I was created to do. People read my vision statement and told me it was "too much," that it was "too big," and some even accused me of "trying to change the world." I felt like they told me my baby was ugly! Some people did not even believe what I had written was divinely inspired or my destiny. Shocking, right? But guess what . . . I did not die of shame or embarrassment like I thought I would. I now knew *who* I was, so I kept speaking my dreams aloud, believing in them instead of my circumstances. I was not deterred or swayed by what others said. I persevered and kept moving forward.

I learned a valuable lesson during this crazy period. My looking crazy was not about me. This was another boot camp designed by my Creator uniquely for me. The courage to be crazy was a test to see if I was trustworthy—could I be trusted with a water-walking, giant-slaying, history-making destiny? Did my destiny mean more to me than people's opinions? Would I sacrifice my reputation and my comfort zones for all I believed? I learned I needed to care more about my destiny than I did about myself. I needed to care more for the approval of my Creator than I did for other people's. I learned to perform only for the audience of One—even if I did look a bit crazy. This was all a part of my ongoing boot camp—small missions given to test my resolve to be and do all I was created to. I believe all of heaven cheered that day as I ran around looking crazy, speaking truth that would lead me to fulfill my destiny.

During one of my first scary acts of "speaking it out loud," I stood on a stage in a small church in Elk Grove, California, in front of about a hundred women. We had an amazing two days together at a Courage Conference where I challenged them to be all they were created to be. After it was over, I announced to them that we would meet in one week and that I would have for them a six-week workbook called the *Uniqueness Assessment*. That may not sound very crazy to you, but to me, it was beyond crazy because I had not written a single word of that assessment! It remained unwritten except in my heart. I was scared to death when I said that aloud. The words flew out of my mouth. It was crazy! I'd had the title of that workbook several years prior, but I had not had the courage, nor did I believe I had the time, to sit down and write it with all we had going on. But on that day, on that stage in front of those women, I knew that they needed that assessment, that encouragement, that vehicle to move them from where they were to where they were supposed to be. So I said it aloud, and it was birthed in the heavens. Speaking it aloud (plus the thought of letting down those precious, courageous women) gave me the courage to sit down and write all night long for days at a time. That same assessment is the *Uniquely You* workbook, now published and ready for future water walkers.

I cannot adequately explain what happens in the spiritual realm when we give words to the secret dreams of our hearts. The most amazing and supernatural things happen when we speak aloud the dreams and destinies we believe are deposited deep within us—crazy things happen as we see them fulfilled!

Birthing Our Dreams

I believe there is an intimate time with our Creator when dreams are too precious and new to share. A time of pregnancy, if you will. They need to remain hidden away in our hearts until they and we have the time to grow and mature into them, until we believe in them and long to see them fulfilled.

Babies must be born. They cannot stay hidden forever. A restlessness sets in just as it does for an expectant mother and father. You are impatient, ready for things to happen. You are no longer satisfied with the secret of the dream, and though you are scared to death, you want to share it with the world. You are willing to risk being called crazy or being misunderstood.

I believe all of heaven smiles when you finally have the courage to be you.

Undaunted, you are ready for your marching orders—for your water-walking, giant-slaying, history-making destiny. You do not care what others may say or even if all hell is trying to silence you. You are courageous—even bold—though you may look a bit crazy. Keep speaking those dreams into being. Your Creator is on your side. He is not setting you up for failure or trying to embarrass you. If He put a dream inside of you, be confident that He intends to fulfill it.

Do you feel pregnant with possibilities? Are you restless to begin? If so, maybe your Creator is ready to start moving heaven and earth's resources to fulfill them. Write down all the seeds of destiny that have been deposited within you. Maybe, just maybe, it is time for you to speak up. Confidently begin to share your dreams with others. It does not matter whether they cheer you on or tell you you're crazy. Your job is to speak and believe. It is impossible to remain silent when you believe you have been created on purpose for a purpose. It would be like trying to keep a baby from being born. Impossible. Your words and belief are powerful forces that cause heaven and earth to move.

Shout it aloud, do not hold back.
Raise your voice like a trumpet.

Isaiah 58:1 NIV

These words were written thousands of years ago but are still relevant today. Can you feel their urgency? The world is waiting for you to fulfill your destiny.

Stumbling along on my own journey, trying daily to find the courage to be the me I was created to be, I found out why birthing our dreams is so important. When you are being the you who you were created to be, people notice. They may think you are crazy at first, but if you do not quit, if you do not give up, then they begin to long for more in their lives and entertain the idea that they may have a water-walking, giant-slaying, history-making destiny too. You being you gives them the courage to believe that they were also created on purpose for a purpose, which is also part of your destiny.

Looking back, I shudder to think where I would have been if I had not chosen to believe my Creator for the truth about me, my life, and my circumstances. I admit there were days when I wavered with doubt, flirted with indecision, and cried a bucket of tears—but I never gave up. I never stopped believing. I pray with all my heart for you to do the same.

I challenge you. Dare to dream, dare to imagine the impossible becoming possible in your life, then take courage and speak it out loud. You are called beloved. You have a place to belong. You were created on purpose for a purpose. Believe it. Shout it from the rooftops or to anyone who will listen. Risk being seen as crazy. What do you really have to lose . . . except fulfilling your dreams?

CHAPTER 14

Clues to Your Destiny

By now, you may be restless and ready to know the details of your destiny. I know I was. I did not think I could wait a moment longer to begin doing whatever it was I was created to do. I wanted to jump in headfirst. However, the process took longer than I would have designed. Instead of a complete detailed how-to version of my world-changing destiny, I received clues much like bread-crumbs left on my path to purpose. The first one came once again from my child-hood dreams and desires.

Marriage, Mom, and Missionary

When I moved from Mississippi to the San Francisco Bay Area in 1992, I was thirty-two years old and completely unprepared for the differences in the two geographical areas. *Culture shock* was not a term I knew. I had never given much thought about California, or specifically the "Bay Area," as those who live there call it. This place seemed like a faraway, foreign land. At this particular moment in my story, all I cared about was moving to that foreign land, far away from my home, because my soon-to-be husband was already living and working there. I gave no thought to my destiny; I just wanted to be wherever he was. Because of our upcoming wedding day, I was giddy about leaving my home and the beautiful, hospitable place I was raised in called "the South." As I packed my bags, I was not contemplating my identity or giving much thought to my destiny. I was just dreaming dreams of happily ever after with my handsome new husband, Michael, and my then-eleven-year-old son, Austin. I was so excited for the three of us to begin our new life together as a family.

On the much anticipated day of our departure, I was gleefully saying my goodbyes (and I do mean gleefully) at the airport. Mother, father, brothers, sisters, and in-laws were all there, struggling to let us go gracefully. My mom was the last in line. She hugged me longer than she usually did. She is not much of a touchy-feely person, so I was a little surprised. As I attempted to untangle myself from her embrace, she let me break away only slightly so that she could look into my eyes. I wondered if my mom had ever held my gaze for that long. Her eyes were saying something to me that she had difficulty expressing with words. She clung to me again, silently crying tears as her oldest baby was about to fly far away from the comfortable nest she was raised in. I broke her grip and gaze. I was so anxious to begin my new life. I picked up my suitcase and followed my husband and my son toward the tarmac to begin our new journey.

Before I could escape, my mom finally found words for the truth that was in her heart and eyes. She touched my shoulder one last time. "California will be your mission field." She stated this fact with great conviction. I turned, looking over my shoulder, wondering who in the world she was speaking to. Oh! It was me! What in the world was she talking about? Mission field? I shook my head and ran for the airplane.

I did not realize it for many years, but that day, that moment, those words may have come from my mother's mouth, but they were a declaration of my destiny. Those words would lay buried in my heart for years until the perfect moment when my Creator would resurrect them and remind me of their origin. My marriage was the vehicle used to transition me to a place I never would have chosen: California.

I smile now as I remember my mom's words. She was remembering something I had long forgotten—a promise I made at a very young age to travel the world to tell people in faraway places about a God who loves them. There were only two things I wanted to be when I grew up, a mom and a missionary. One carried no more weight in my heart than the other. Actually, those aspirations were much more specific and extremely well thought out for a child as young as I was when I could first articulate them. I wanted to be a mom of ten kids. I also wanted to be a very specific kind of missionary: a foreign missionary in a place far away from Mississippi. This desire was so real and compelling that I had told everyone of my plan by the time I was nine years old. I did not once worry about someone thinking I was crazy. Nope, I was confident.

To prove my commitment and belief in my dream, I walked the aisle at my church one Sunday morning, declaring to my pastor and all who were in attendance the seriousness of my intent. At nine years of age, I was certain of my destiny—marriage, mom, and missionary. As I planned out my life in my little-girl mind, I would marry the man of my dreams and take him, along with my children, to faraway, exotic lands like Africa or South America. I was going to major in home economics, and I would teach the indigent population how to cook and care for their homes and families. That was my plan, my little-girl dream: marriage, mom, and missionary.

Fast-forward twenty years to when I stood at the airplane departure gate gazing at my mother as the airplane's engine drowned out her declaration. I was divorced. A single mom leaving my home state for the first time, at the ripe old age of thirty-two, to marry for the second time a man I loved madly, accompanied by my eleven-year-old son, who I would gladly sacrifice anything for but this marriage. We were not headed to the mission field, and there were no daughters in sight. At that point, I had never traveled outside the United States and didn't even have a passport. My life had not turned out quite like I dreamed. In fact, I had not thought about my desire to be a foreign missionary in years. So at that particular moment in my history, my mother's declaration seemed ludicrous to me.

My expectancy and excitement regarding my new life in California were not in vain. I had no preconceived ideas about California one way or the other. I was delighted with my new home and the people I met. Everyone loved my Southern accent and my Southern cooking, even though they thought being from "the South" meant San Diego. They also thought my belief in God was "cute." We made friends that felt like family, and I birthed two more boys. I loved our life in the Bay Area. I did not know it at the time, but the Bay Area and the environment I found myself in was a strategic plan devised by my Creator just for me and my destiny.

On my forty-first year on this earth, I began asking the questions *Who am I* and *Why am I here?* I had begun my journey of purpose. My childbearing years were over, my tubes tied to ensure it. I had three biological sons I loved madly, and I was happy. My husband had a fabulous job, and I had even gotten a passport to go to Mexico for a vacation. Yet as I described earlier, I was restless to find my purpose. Then God asked me that question, "Do you have the courage to be you—the you I created?" He nudged me forward into my future and brought me memories of the past. Very specific memories, showing me the little girl I once was, and the day I stopped being me. However, months later, more memories came. Memories not just about who I was but what I longed to do. I remembered my passion to travel the world to faraway places, like Africa and South America, where I would testify of a loving Creator and my long-buried desire for more children. In that moment I felt the whispered words, *You will travel the world, and you will have daughters.*

Let me explain the daughter desire.

When I was a teenage girl, I had friends of mine who called their moms their best friends. They told their moms all their secrets. Their moms were their confidants. I met another friend who told me her grandmother was that person. She showed me a book of letters that her grandmother had written her on each of her birthdays from ages one to sixteen, having them bound in a book.

I wanted that.

My mom and I have that now (me at sixty-two and her at eighty-two). However, when I was growing up, I was one of three kids. My mom parented three kids under the age of four when she was twenty-four years old. She was the most amazing mom, but during my junior high and high school years, she was not my best friend. However, that was when I started having the strongest of desires to have daughters, not because I wanted girls, but because I wanted relationship—close, intimate, authentic relationship with someone I could totally be myself with.

So when God whispered to me I would have daughters after birthing three sons who held my heart in their hands, I felt seen by the God of the universe and realized He planted that desire for far bigger purposes than the children I would birth. It would be for girls—and a few boys—who did not have a mother to love them, protect them, and believe in them.

I felt pregnant! Pregnant with possibilities, pregnant with the impossible! I did not understand the ramifications or exactly what it all meant, but I did realize my dreams were not dead. They were just buried.

Our Dreams Are a Roadmap

I learned something very important about our Creator and dreams that day. Our little-girl or little-boy dreams deposited in us before time began are very often a roadmap to our destiny, a destiny that time does not negate or erase. No matter how much time it takes, our Creator longs to awaken and fulfill the dreams He gave us—even the ones we have forgotten from our childhood. Looking back to our childhood dreams and desires, we can find clues to our identity and destiny because they were there before life, our choices, and the choices of others intervened. It seems not to matter to our Creator how long it takes or what has transpired in our life; He remains in the business of fulfilling the dreams He gave.

By the time my dreams and desires were resurrected, I had walked out on a marriage, was divorced, and now married for the second time. I did not have a passport and had never traveled to a faraway place. I never took home economics or ever testified aloud about a loving Creator. I had three sons who I adored and no longer longed for daughters, but I could not wait to love the women they would one day marry and call them "daughter." But God kept the memories coming of what I loved to do as a little girl and caused a flicker of desire to ignite in my spirit. I remembered loving being on a stage, and I felt my Creator say, *You will speak to many.* I remembered writing poems sitting in a tree, and I felt the words, *You will write a book.* I loved to lead teams and felt my Creator say, *You will lead an army.* I wanted to be a cheerleader ever since I attended my first Ole Miss football game and had been one in the fourth grade at Green Elementary School and again when I was a senior in high school at Callaway High in Jackson, Mississippi. As I remembered this passion, I heard that small whisper of my Creator saying, *You will be an encourager and cheerleader for many.* I remembered picking friends that no one else picked when I was very young in elementary school before I stopped being me. My Creator told me, *You will be a voice for the voiceless.*

I did not know the "how" of it all. However, I was perfectly content just knowing that my little-girl dreams and desires were not forgotten, that *I* was not forgotten. This gave me the courage to open myself up to the possibility of the impossible. I was *going* to travel the world, I was *going* to speak from a stage, I was *going* to write a book, I was *going* to lead an army (to where I had no clue), and I was *going* to have daughters! It was my destiny, and all the clues came from my childhood dreams and passions.

What about you? What were your little-girl or little-boy dreams and desires? Do you remember what you wanted to be when you grew up? Have you become that? Are there any dreams and desires that have not come to pass that maybe you gave up on and buried prematurely? Ask your Creator to help you remember and resurrect them. Ask Him for clues from your childhood. Pay attention to the titles you wanted to have and the jobs you wanted to do; they may be clues to your identity and destiny.

I entertained many career options along the way. At one point, I wanted to be a chiropractor and later an interior decorator. Social worker, journalist, and psychiatrist also made the list for different reasons. As I reflected on these interests, they eventually gave me clues to who I was and what I was created to do. Chiropractor because I believe in natural healing; decorator because I love tranquil, beautiful spaces; social worker because I love to help people; journalist because I love to write; and psychiatrist because I am fascinated by human behavior. Mom because I am a nurturer. Missionary because I had experienced the love of my Maker. Cheerleader because I am an encourager. I may not have had the job titles, but in those interests I was discovering who I was and what I was created to do. On this journey, I realized the little-girl dreams and desires of my heart were different from job titles. The job titles and careers I was interested in were just more breadcrumbs left by my Creator.

When I first started this journey of uncovering my identity and discovering my destiny, I did not even remember my childhood dreams. If I had, I would have probably shrugged them off as mere childhood fantasies. I had no idea I was settling for less than what was planned for me.

Friends, be encouraged! Let me be the one to speak this truth to your mind, heart, soul, and spirit. Your Creator has not forgotten your childhood dreams and the desires of your heart. If He placed them there, He intends to fulfill them. Like me, you may have to let go of your preconceived ideas of "how" and let your Creator orchestrate the fulfillment of them all. You will not be disappointed. I am praying right now that you have the courage to consult your Creator and ask Him to bring to memory any dreams, passions, careers, or job titles He placed inside of you before time began. Journal them all to see if they are breadcrumbs leading to your water-walking, giant-slaying, history-making destiny! Listen to your spirit and the still, small voice inside. Listen for clues from the past. They may just help you change the world.

CHAPTER 15

What Is Your Passion?

I wish I could tell you that after my long-buried dreams for world travel, speaking on stages, writing books, and having daughters were resurrected, the restlessness I described earlier ended. It did not. Not only did it continue, but it increased! I was ready for some action. I needed to be doing something!

I felt compelled to sign up for a class at church that proclaimed that I would discover my "spiritual gifts," though I had no idea what in the world a spiritual gift was. However, the idea was exciting because I believed I was not born with any natural talents and there was nothing gifted about me unless you counted talking.

On the very first night of class, I almost quit! The first small-group question after the video finished playing was posed: "What are you passionate about?" I tried to remain calm. I stared at the blank piece of paper. I felt like I needed to breathe into a paper bag. The instructions were to write down your reflections on that question, and then you would be asked to share your thoughts with the group. That caused a panic attack since I had not yet overcome my fear of public speaking. Sitting in a chair surrounded by fifteen other people qualified as such. I did not want to share! I did not have anything to share.

I had just told my husband the week before how I envied his passion for golf. He would go out in the cold and pouring down rain just to hit a bucket of balls! Nothing could get me out in the cold and rain. Nothing. My passion? The question loomed. I did not have an answer.

My anxiety mounted as the group began putting their pens down. Each person's paper was full of their passions. My paper was blank and wet from my sweaty palms. I was dreading my turn. I had no idea what I would say. For some reason, it felt hideously wrong to say I did not have a passion. The process began, and around the table we went. I prayed I would be last. I started getting an icky feeling in the pit of my stomach, the same one I'd had when I was called to the principal's office as a little girl—impending embarrassment and humiliation. Finally, my name was called. "Jenny? What are you passionate about?" I felt like I was going to faint.

The facilitator must have recognized my anguish because she embellished the question a bit more by saying, "What could you sit and do for hours and hours?" First of all, this was so the wrong question for me—I do not sit for hours and hours and "do" anything! Sitting still is not one of my talents or abilities. My mind was filled with random thoughts like these as I stalled for time.

Then a new phenomenon occurred. I was struck mute! Rarely have I been rendered speechless. I could not say a word, but tears welled in my eyes, threatening to spill over onto my already perspiration-soaked blank piece of paper. I felt like I was back in grade school. Everyone was staring at me. Three seconds of silence can be agonizing.

Then suddenly, from somewhere deep inside of me, without any rehearsed thought, my mouth opened, and out burst the cry of my heart. "I am passionate about everything! I have a passionate opinion about everything and nothing. I am so passionate that I wear myself out on a daily basis!"

The facilitator smiled a knowing smile. I wondered if she knew something I did not. As the words left my mouth and the sound traveled up to my ears, I knew in my spirit it was truth. My problem was not a lack of passion, it was an overwhelming abundance of it. It was what I had been criticized for most all my life.

I shocked myself. How can you be passionate about everything but no *one* thing? I say yes to any and everything anyone asks me to do. My hand shoots up to volunteer of its own accord. In my spirit, I am screaming *pick me*—for anything. I did not know if I was truly passionate about everything or if I just liked to be included.

I left the class feeling more restless and ordinary than ever. What was I to do with this new self-awareness? The facilitator had given us a homework assignment. We were to ask someone we trusted for help defining or, in my case, narrowing down our passions. Who would I ask? With this question, the possibility of embarrassment or humiliation reached an all-time high. I almost quit my journey of purpose right then and there. I was holding on tight to my identity.

I am so glad I did not quit because my answer was close by—my bed! With the least likely person—my husband! When I returned home from class that evening, my husband was in bed watching television. I burst into the room and interrupted his favorite program on TV, golf! If the man cannot play golf, he watches it. Bursting into tears, I flung myself on his chest, explaining my lack of a specific passion.

"Passionate about everything isn't an answer!" I blubbered. He was surprisingly patient with me since self-awareness is so not his thing. I told him I had to have someone help me narrowly define my passions, someone who knew me and loved me. Though he qualified as that person, I never once entertained the notion that he might volunteer his services. Calm and confident man that he is, he took the now-soggy homework paper I was clutching in my hand, skimmed over the hundreds of questions, threw it on the floor, and with great wisdom, said, "I know what you are passionate about."

Time stood still. Hope welled up inside of me. Could it be this easy? The man who loves and knows me better than anyone in the entire world—could he really have my answer? My husband delivered his answer with no fanfare: "Your girlfriends. They are always calling you, asking for your advice and encouragement, asking for your help with children, husbands, marriage, jobs, and arguments. You are the 'Dear Abby' of our neighborhood." He lovingly concluded, "You are passionate about all women, as well as friends, family, neighbors, and complete strangers! And you are equally passionate about your children."

Be still, my heart. He was right!

I did have a passion, and my husband had uncovered it for me! Somewhere along the path of my life, my Creator had given me a love and passion for women and for all issues that affect them. Paradoxically, I had spent most of my life hanging out with guys. My best friends have always been guys. I really did not like "girls." I wanted them to be more like men—less drama, less talking, more doing!

This profound discovery of my passion, coupled with my resurrected dream to have daughters, led me to action. With my knees knocking and all the courage I could muster, I opened my home weekly to a small group of women. I thought I had died and gone to heaven. I was doing something! My restlessness subsided. This group of women became the first Righteous Girlfriend Group (RGG). I was passionate about having them in my home every week. We shared our hearts, our lives, and our journeys to God. These women ultimately became my spiritual daughters; my dream was fulfilled, or so I thought. This was my first taste of my destiny—of being and doing all I was created to be and do. It was highly addictive.

Defining my passion was the most difficult for me, so I hope I am making your journey of purpose easier. Passion was so nebulous to me. I could recognize it in others but not in myself. I did a little research on the word to help clarify exactly what a *passion* is. Webster calls it "a strong liking or desire for or devotion to some activity, object, or concept."[11] Dictionary.com defines it as "any powerful or compelling emotion or feeling, such as love or hate."[12] Ah, simplicity!

Just ask yourself, *What do I strongly like, love, hate, or totally get emotional about?*

My thought for you as we end this chapter is that you will begin to feel a restlessness in your spirit to "do something." I pray that God will reveal to you the specific passion He deposited in you long before time began. I pray that you will have a new divine awareness of the people and situations that move you to compassion. I pray that compassion will lead you straight to action in spite of your fears and circumstances. I pray you will consult your Creator daily to be reminded of who you are and the inheritance you hold.

You were created on purpose for a purpose, and your passions hold a clue!

CHAPTER 16

Looking Back to Generations Before

I am just so excited! How I long to look deep into your eyes and tell you that your life matters. I long for you to know that you are created on purpose for a purpose. You, your life, and your destiny are to be a history maker, world changer, water walker, and giant slayer! Whether you realize it or not, whether you are intentional about it or not, you are impacting lives and situations daily. Good and bad, positive and negative.

Does that stop you in your tracks? It does for me. It actually boggles my mind when I take the time to ponder and contemplate the hugeness of that concept! My little life, decisions, and choices greatly affect the people around me. I can wrap my brain around believing I may have some impact on my immediate family or friends—but complete strangers or people who have not even been born yet? I did not give much thought to this until recently when I realized how the destinies of the people who had gone before me have shaped and contributed to my own life and destiny.

I got "the call" at 6:00 a.m. on March 13, 2005. I had been waiting on this call ever since the day I moved to California. When you leave home, away from all those you call family and friends, you *know* that one day you will get "the call" that comes in the middle of the night and drives you to your knees. The one that tells you someone you have loved is gone, that his or her life has come to an end. Knowing it and expecting it does not lessen the pain when you answer it. It does not even lessen when the end is welcomed because suffering has ceased. My Mimi was gone.

I told you her name was Elizabeth, and she was adopted from an orphanage. On that spring day, her spirit left her worn-out body, although her mind had been gone for a while. She was ninety-two years old. As her obituary chronicled, she was survived by two daughters, seven grandchildren, twelve great-grandchildren, and one great-great-grandchild. Funny how they sum up a life in the newspaper that way—survived by, gone before her, born, lived, died. It struck me as funny when I first read it; then I was sad because they were talking about my grandmother. My Mimi's life was so much more than a paragraph in the back of a newspaper. Her life and her choices have impacted so many people, including mine. I was determined that she was going to have a grander send off than that. Much to my surprise, my passion led me straight to action. I was going to give her eulogy. It did not matter that I had never done a eulogy before. I just knew in my heart it was what I had to do.

My original plan had been to visit my Mimi when I made my annual pilgrimage home to Mississippi. I wanted her to have a clear mind, just for a moment, so I could look into her eyes, hold her hand, and tell her how much her life, her choices, her decisions, and her obedience had impacted my life. I wanted her to know how her love for God had affected my identity and now my destiny. I wanted to thank her. I wanted to tell her that all the hardships she endured, all the rejection and pain, all the battles she fought were not in vain—they were for me, for us, and for the generations that followed her. I am quite sure she never contemplated her choices in light of how they would affect those that would come after her. However, they did, and I wanted her to know that. Sadly, she left this world before I ever had the opportunity to tell her all the things stored in my heart. I could not leave the eulogy to the young pastor who had only known her as an old woman who had lost her mind. When he met her, she had not been my Mimi in a long time and instead was a scared little girl trapped in an old woman's body. She spent a lot of time remembering the past.

I am laughing and crying as I remember her. Even without her mind, she was a force until the day she died. My mom and aunt went to choose her casket before she died at the prompting of the doctor since she "didn't have much time left." However, he did not know my Mimi. No one told her what to do or when to do it—especially when to exit this world. After selecting her casket and planning her funeral, she lingered for another seven days. She was a fighter and a giant slayer until the very end. Five feet tall, 110 pounds soaking wet, and full of spit and vinegar was a common description of my Mimi. Still, she was scared to death to fly in an airplane—she never did—and to the day she died, she hated being left alone or in the dark.

She was such a contradiction. My aunt told me that once, as a young girl, my Mimi ditched school, put on her roller skates, and hooked a rope to a car so she could skate around town. Fearless one moment and frightened little girl the next. She was little but strong. Humble yet willful. She was not going anywhere until she was good and ready! I told everyone at the funeral that she probably lingered on this earth, waiting for someone in heaven to go get my "Daddy-Jay" (her husband) off the lawn mower somewhere in the back forty of heaven so he would be waiting to welcome her as she made her entrance into heaven. My Daddy-Jay. He had been gone for almost twenty-three years, and my Mimi missed him every one of those days. The two of them could make you believe in true love, fairy tales, and soul mates. I have the original love poems my Mimi wrote to her man. Their love for each other impacted all the lives they touched.

Here I stood on a stage and spoke to people. Another dream was fulfilled, or so I thought.

Interestingly enough, the first people to hear my Mimi's eulogy were little kids. The day I received that phone call was a Sunday morning, and I was scheduled to teach the children's class at church. The story I was to teach was about David and Goliath. The focus word for the kids was *courage*. I was an emotional mess. Everything that morning reminded me of my Mimi—especially this particular story. Standing before the kids, I began to tell the story of David facing the giant. I did not have to embellish the story to hold their attention. Kids just love hearing how a shepherd boy defeated a nine-foot giant armed only with a little slingshot, some common river rocks, and an enormous belief in his God.

As I finished telling the story, I promised these children that God would never ask them to fight a nine-foot giant with a slingshot! I did promise them, however, that at some time in their life—and probably more than once—He would ask them to do something that was very difficult, very scary, and could only be accomplished with an enormous belief in their Creator and all the courage they could muster. Every adult in the room nodded their agreement.

My little grandmother had to fight a giant, but the giant was not a nine-foot-tall Philistine. It was the giant of prejudice and racism in the Deep South during the early 1940s and 1950s before there was a civil rights movement. My Mimi impacted her world in a mighty way, including complete strangers and unborn children, by crossing the literal tracks and teaching those called less-than about the love of hers and their Creator. She invited people into her home that did not look like her and served them. Not only did she serve them, she called many "family." For that and more, she had a cross burned in her yard and was thrown out of her church. At my grandfather's funeral years ago, an old African American gentleman shuffled into the funeral parlor to tell me what my grandparents meant to him. I will never forget his words: "If it wasn't for Miss Liz and Mr. J. D., I would have never known the Lord Jesus as my Savior, 'cause they had come to teach the children."

What a eulogy, what a testimony . . . what a legacy.

By the time I was born, my Mimi's giant-slaying days were over. I only knew her as my grandmother. My great-grandmother Eleanor rescued my Mimi from an orphanage from an identity that said she was unwanted and had no value to a destiny that literally changed the lives of individuals in her world because she chose to fight an injustice that many others chose to ignore. I have received blessings in my life that are a direct correlation to my Mimi's love of others and her Creator and the actions of her compassion. The ceiling of her life became the floor on which I stand, gazing into my destiny. Oh, how I pray my children and grandchildren will be able to say the same of me!

It completely boggles my mind how looking back through the lens of time can bring such clarity to my destiny. I shake my head in wonder and cry with the realization that my destiny started with a woman born in the late 1800s. A woman named Eleanor Glass, who I called "Granny" but is of no blood relation to me. A woman whose wedding band I now claim as my own, who fought to rescue one child from an orphanage, bestowing the identity of daughter and the name Elizabeth upon her. It was Elizabeth who, because of that identity, went on to rescue and set free individuals of another color whom her peers said were unworthy, invaluable, and throwaways at that time. I called her Mimi, and I also wear her ring as my own—she changed her own world. The rescued often become rescuers. These two ordinary women and their courageous choices have radically influenced my life and my destiny long after their deaths.

Little did I know that I would one day have daughters who I did not birth, who would bear the names of these two women. Little did I know that I, too, would fight injustices too big for me and rescue children who would need a home.

Friends, our destinies are often in our DNA and our histories! There is deposited within us a desire to matter—it is part of our identity and destiny. That desire is for us to be water walkers, giant slayers, and history makers. The clues in our past point to the exact nature of that destiny. Are there doctors, lawyers, pastors, firemen, police chiefs, moms, or teachers in your past? Is there a tendency for people in your family to be risk-takers or facilitators of other people's dreams?

Ask family members who are still around if they can help you connect any dots. Talk with the oldest family members and ask them to tell you the family stories. Write them all down. Celebrate those who have gone before you and mine their lives for the treasures that can make you rich.

Do not be discouraged if you do not have access to the people or stories before you. Consult your Creator—He has all your answers. If you do not have a family tree that looks like mine, you may be the first water walker, giant slayer, and history maker in your family! Your children and grandchildren will thank you.

We are on this planet to change the world, one individual at a time. Just do it! It will take courage—action in the face of our fear. For such a time as this, you were born. You being you matters. It matters to this generation and to the one to come! My desire for you as you end this chapter is that you will begin to consider your legacy. How high will the ceiling you leave for the next generation be? Ignore the "what-ifs" and the "how will I ever" taunts of the giant. You will be provided with all the slingshots and rocks you will ever need. Let your passion propel you into action.

Let your life be the breadcrumbs others will follow to their unique destinies.

CHAPTER 17

Our Unfounded Fears

I hate that I have lived most of my life afraid. Afraid of what others would think, afraid of losing my job, afraid of losing my home, afraid of losing my kids, afraid of losing my breasts, afraid of losing my husband, afraid of being embarrassed, afraid of speaking, afraid of writing, afraid of being used, afraid of going bankrupt, afraid of failing. Afraid of everything. Afraid about nothing.

I once heard that human beings are the only species that can scare themselves. That's me.

Afraid, afraid, afraid.

That is why for so long, I hated the word *courage*. It implied you were going to have to do something you were afraid of. I had avoided that most of my life. I believed courage was a personality trait. Either you had it, or you did not. And I did not have it, nor did I want it. But the further I have walked in this journey of purpose, the more I have come to love the word, for I learned it simply meant *action*. Action I love; it is fear I try to avoid.

Former First Lady Eleanor Roosevelt disagrees with me. She suggested you should "Do one thing every day that scares you."[13] My mind screams, *Why?* But even as I ask the question, I know the answer. Doing something that scares me, something I fear, requires me to choose courage; it requires action on my part. Fear paralyzes me, but courage moves me through its invisible wall. When I break through that wall, a sense of accomplishment and confidence embraces me. After a while, you become accustomed to doing things scared. With experience, you soon realize your fears like your feelings are not true indicators of truth. With enough practice, you will find that you do not even require courage anymore because, at some point in time when you were not even aware, you have become bold. That is when you become dangerous—when you are a full-fledged member of the water-walking, giant-slaying, history-making club.

I have found that fears can even be helpful in identifying your unique world-changing destiny. The very thing that at one time scared me the most was exactly what I was created to do. My dog, Jake, taught me that lesson.

As I mentioned before, Jake was a Labrador retriever. Labs were created on purpose for a purpose—swimming and hunting. They love to get wet and they love to fetch. They are literally made for it. Labs have a thick tail called an otter tail that is designed to propel them through the water at great speed to fetch the ducks their owners shoot out of the sky. Their hair is much like a duck's feathers; it repels water. Getting a Lab soaking wet is a difficult feat. All Labs love water— except Jake. He did not swim or fetch. He was scared to death of the very thing he was created for.

It all started when we gave him a bath as a puppy. Bathing a dog is an unnatural act, but because Jake was being groomed to be a housedog and not a hunter, he needed to smell good if he was to be granted access to our home. On this particular day, Michael, my husband, and my two young sons, Michael-Dean and Ben, were lathering up Jake with rosemary-scented dog soap. Ben was holding Jake while my husband held the water hose. Michael-Dean's job was to turn the water on and off when his dad yelled, "Turn it on!" and "Turn it off!" The directive was shouted, and Michael-Dean turned on the water. When he did, the force of the water whipped the hose out of my husband's soapy hands, hit Jake in the head, and sprayed water all over his poor face. In the process, Ben got soaked, too, so he screamed, causing Jake to run out of the backyard with the entire family in pursuit. When we finally caught him, he was hiding in the neighbor's hedge. We dragged him out by his front legs. The emotional trauma that poor dog endured was severe and long-lasting. Thank heaven my husband and boys were unscathed. Jake never recovered. From that day forward, Jake refused to go near *any* body of water. He would cross to the other side of the street if he saw a puddle or a sprinkler. Swimming? No way. He shook like a leaf if near any type of water.

We tried everything, even throwing him in. (In hindsight, I do not advise this course of action; it only made things worse.) Jake had become afraid of the very thing in which he was created to thrive in. Now, do not feel too sorry for Jake. Though he was not being and doing all he was created to do, he lived a very good, comfortable life. Though he did not swim, he loved riding in the car and was allowed to go most places we went. He loved tennis balls but never got the whole fetch thing. He was terribly afraid of rain, so we let him inside the garage because his big otter tail knocked over everything in the house. Gradually we let him come inside only if he could courageously endure a quick, fragrant bath. (He hated blow dryers as much as water.) He liked barking at the dogs on the television. We did not let him on the couch but got him his own feather bed—which he chewed to pieces if left alone. He seemed happy with his domestication. When he was outside for any length of time, he managed to escape because he did not like to be alone. I think I rescued him seven times from the pound or from one of the neighbors who would graciously take him inside. He was always glad to see me but seemed content to stay where he was as long as other people were around. He liked people better than other dogs; thus, he was never enthusiastic about doggy parks, but he loved our walks on the levee, though he always remained afraid and far from the water. That is, until one day when he was about eight years old—about sixty-two in people years.

We were on our regular daily purpose walk. I had taken Jake to our church, which backs up to the San Francisco Bay, so he could sniff and be off the leash. That day, I was not attuned to Jake's wanderings as I was contemplating my identity and destiny. Suddenly, I saw a quick movement out of the corner of my eye. To my utter amazement, Jake was running, really *running*—like a dog— straight in the direction of a large body of water that had two ducks sitting on it. It is difficult to explain what happened in those few minutes, but I can only describe it as that which Jake was created for. Becoming more powerful than his fear, I saw him gracefully fly through the air and belly flop on the water! It was a thing of pure beauty. Then he started swimming toward the ducks! They started to fly, and he chased them. I do not know who was shocked more: Jake, me, or the ducks! I watched in stunned silence. Jake was swimming.

On this particular day, Jake took courage, and he did it scared.

When Jake finished his swim, he ran to my side. I swear he was smiling, and that big ole fat tail was wagging at a crazy speed. Soaking wet, he shook his entire body, spraying me with water. I sank to the grass and hugged my wet dog. Laughing all alone on the wet grass, I contemplated the divine gift I had just received. It was the gift of watching my dog overcome fear and do the very thing he was created to do—the very thing that his fear had stolen. It was as if time stood still.

A tear slipped down my cheek as I hugged my very courageous dog, and I sensed these words:

> *You are no different from Jake. You, too, have become domesticated. Your fears are unfounded. The very thing you are afraid to do is the very thing I have created you for.*

Now I wept. I knew it was true.

My fears seemed pitiful and small. I feared regret, failure, criticism, and laughter. I realized I only did the things I felt comfortable with and was good at. I was afraid to try anything new because my old enemy—embarrassment—just might come for a visit. I was a forty-something-year-old woman, and the bottom line was that I was afraid to be me. I remembered that bold, passionate little girl and knew that fear was keeping me from fulfilling my destiny. I vowed to walk through my invisible walls of fear so that I could be and do all I was created for. Jake was my inspiration. However, Jake had a natural instinct kick in when he saw the water and ducks; you and I must daily make the intentional choice of courage, of taking action in spite of our fear.

I began to do things that scared me—things that deep inside I longed to do and things that I had done as a child. I volunteered to lead a small group. I publicly shared my testimony. I trained for a sixteen-mile hike to the top of a mountain. I led a group of women to the top of Half Dome in Yosemite National Park. I led a ministry. I spoke on a stage. I taught a class. I organized conferences. I shared my faith. I spoke up. I started a nonprofit organization. I began to write a book.

I practiced being me. And I did it scared.

Cassandra's Example

Beautiful sixteen-year-old Cassandra attended one of our very first Courage Conferences and Uniqueness Assessment Workshops. During the second small group session, I asked if anyone had a courageous story to share. Cassandra raised her hand. She said that during the first week of the Uniqueness Assessment, she was doing her homework, and she came up with a song. She wrote down the words and melody she heard that night. I was so excited when Cassandra shared this that I immediately asked if she would sing it. She quickly said, "No!" We all laughed, and I offered the microphone to someone else.

The next week I arrived early to the group. I was up front as the women were entering. I saw Cassandra's beautiful curly red hair immediately—and she was carrying her guitar! I ran up to her and asked, "Are you going to perform your song?" She shyly smiled and said yes. I could not wait to tell everyone! My heart was pounding. I knew her Creator was delighted because she was about to walk through an invisible wall of fear, and we, her righteous girlfriends who were much older, were getting a front-row seat at this incredible display. I was so nervous for her.

Cassandra took the microphone and told us her little-girl story. When she was six years old, she was to perform at her first piano recital. Taking her seat before the massive instrument, she looked out into the sea of faces and froze. She could not remember her song. She walked away from the piano. Her piano teacher sent her back out to overcome her fear and try again. Still, she froze. We all held our breaths as we remembered similar fears. At six, she walked off the stage and away from her destiny. She told us that she had not stood in front of an audience on a stage alone since that day. What courage she displayed! We all held our breaths as she put her guitar in place. Tears were already flowing down my cheeks. Her courage and her fear were both palpable. I whispered a prayer as she began to sing the song she had written, titled "Lord, Move My Feet."

Not a soul dared to take a breath. Cassandra and, I believe, all the angels in heaven sang together. When she finished, I did not detect a dry eye in the room. She smiled the same smile Jake did. The entire room got to their feet, clapping and cheering, celebrating the fact that it did not take Cassandra thirty years to courageously face her fears as it had for most of us. Another incredible gift. Another timeless moment when I had the opportunity to watch a courageous water walker step out of her boat onto the water. At that moment, I prayed for my children. I prayed they would learn this lesson long before I had. I had wasted so much time.

Cassandra's mom approached her at the end of the evening and asked, "What if you had left your guitar in the car?" What I think she really meant was, "What if your fear had won? What if you had chosen to stay in your boat?"

Fast forward till today. Cassandra leads worship at a church. Has graduated college with an art degree. Has traveled to Tanzania with Courage Worldwide and painted murals at Courage House, and taught art to our girls there. She has continued to lead worship and paint on stages—fearless.

Friends, it is time for you to face your fears, get out of the boat of the known, and courageously walk into the unknown. This is where you will discover your world-changing destiny.

In my own journey of purpose, I have come to believe there are only a few things we should fear:

. . . that you will settle for less than you were created for.

. . . that you will give up and quit too soon.

. . . that you will never attempt anything great.

. . . that no one will ever notice you were here.

Let those fears propel you into your destiny. Take one step, any step, for it is far better to dare mighty things and experience defeat than to sit on the sidelines of life, never attempting anything. It seems that President and Mrs. Roosevelt agree, and both knew a thing or two about doing things that are scary.

> It is not the critic who counts; not the man who points out how the strong man stumbled or where the doer of deeds could have done them better. The credit belongs to the man who is actually in the arena; whose face is marred by dust and sweat and blood; who strives valiantly; who errs and comes short again and again, because there is no effort without error and shortcoming; who does actually try to do the deed; who knows the great enthusiasm, the great devotions and spends himself on a worthy cause; who, at the worst, if he fails at least fails while daring greatly. Far better it is to dare mighty things, to win glorious triumphs even though checkered by failure, than to rank with those poor spirits who neither enjoy nor suffer much because they live in the gray twilight that knows neither victory nor defeat.
>
> —Theodore Roosevelt[14]

I Get to Be Me!

*M*y birthday wish from my forty-third birthday, penned by Maya Angelou, is on the original birthday card tucked right inside my Bible. I read it often.

> *"Today I wish for you one perfect moment when you are utterly*
> *yourself, when you are convinced you are God's own child . . .*
> *when you realize that everything is within your grasp."*

I am still enamored with these words. A moment, a perfect moment, when you are utterly yourself. I love the sound of that. I just get to be me. Sounds so simple—so freeing—but for some reason, so difficult for so many of us. In the midst of seeking clues for our unique destiny, we must take time just to be who we were created to be. We must learn to love and enjoy ourselves because we cannot love another until we love ourselves.

This is what our focus will be in this chapter—those moments when you catch a glimpse of your true self, clues to who you are and what you are supposed to be doing. The moments when you feel free. When everything is effortless. When you find your sweet spot.

I was reminded of Maya's words during an encounter with a three-year-old named Kayla. She literally plopped in my lap, completely startling me. "An angel" was my first thought. "Delightful" was my second. In that moment, I would have told you that her arrival was unplanned, maybe even random, if I believed in such things. However, I would have been wrong. Time would reveal that this landing was intentional and full of purpose. This delightful, pint-sized angel would not be simply a gift for the moment but a tender reminder of someone I lost a long time ago.

I was alone and operating in full mommy mode prior to this divine lap landing. My middle son, Michael-Dean, had band practice at our church. His first public guitar performance was scheduled for the next evening, and I had the mom task of carpooling. I comforted myself with the thought of two uninterrupted hours of inspired reading to pass the time while I waited. I had just claimed my seat on the floor with a few other carpool-weary moms and was about to get lost in my book when a swirling blond vision caught my eye. Without warning but to my utter delight, this lovely child plopped into my lap.

My senses were overwhelmed as her strawberry-scented hair covered my face and obscured my view. I was literally wrapped in angel hair. Her tiny hand caressed my face, and she laughed as she freed her hair from mine. What came into view was clearly a beautiful angel masquerading as a three-year-old only inches from my face. Without hesitation or a proper introduction, she threw her arms around my neck and stared intently into my eyes. With stillness uncommon to children her age, she held my gaze, hypnotizing me. Though neither of us spoke, we communicated perfectly in the silence. An eternity later, she broke the spell when she asked, "Will you be my friend?" Though it was the most ordinary of questions, the words were spoken with such confidence, eloquence, and sophistication that I felt I was being chosen for a great honor. My yes delighted her so much that she hugged me as if she had known me her entire life. Captivated, I fell completely and madly in love. I spent the rest of the evening willingly engrossed in this child-angel and her world. Joy bubbled up from my soul and tangibly displayed itself as tears in my eyes. I giggled (which is much different from laughing) out loud, for I knew without a doubt that I had just been ambushed from the ordinary and thrown headfirst into the extraordinary.

In retelling the story, I am still amazed at how this little pint-sized girl plopped so confidently into my lap. It still astonishes me that she did so without any apparent fear of rejection. I guess being so young, she had not yet felt the sting of that particular emotion, and I never wanted her to. So I wrapped my arms tightly around her, burying my nose deep in her hair while she talked nonstop. As she shared her angel secrets, I noticed a serious little boy hovering nearby. I was about to speak to him when Kayla whispered in my ear, as three-year-old little girls do, that he was her big brother. By the look on his face, it was obvious he was extremely wary of my close encounter with his little sister. Suddenly, with great drama, he cupped his hands around his mouth and loudly proclaimed, "Stranger! Stranger!" to anyone who would listen—especially me. His body language actually screamed, "Danger! Danger!" But my little angel ignored her brother's warning, possessively wrapping her arms tighter around my neck. Her love for me was not cautious but extremely extravagant. I felt bathed in it, even if her big brother was not amused.

The room we were in was large and had been cleared of all chairs for my son's concert the next evening. There were not many people in the room, but there were more on the stage, which was covered with instruments, amplifiers, and nervous adolescents eager yet scared to death to perform in their first concert. No one paid any attention to Kayla and me—except her brothers. Another brother had shown up by this time. This one, however, was not fazed at all by my love affair with his little sister. He was content to sit beside us, quietly reading a book. The concerned oldest brother continued to hover nearby just in case Kayla needed to be rescued. We all listened to the band play. The music was exceptionally beautiful. This place and time seemed enchanted.

After a while, in spite of our mutual love, my little angel got antsy and needed to move her body through space. As quickly as she entered my lap, she left it. But before I could feel the ache of missing her, she reappeared in front of me. This time not to sit with me but to perform for me. I was honored and thrilled! My little angel turned into a dancer and began spinning in circles, round and round and round. She never once got dizzy, a feat she was quite proud of and one I remembered accomplishing myself long, long ago. She danced uninhibited to the young band's music, confident they played only for her. When they paused, she ran as fast as she could across the room, flying, so she claimed, with arms outstretched, jumping in the air like a ballerina. I clapped and cheered loudly. I never once took my eyes off her. She kept looking at me, making sure I was looking at her. I was her audience of one, and my undivided attention mattered greatly to her. My delight in her grew as she performed with an abandon common only to three-year-olds. She danced with all her heart, and suddenly I had the desire to do the same. But, like the mature adult I was, I suppressed the urge and remained anchored to the floor.

Several times during my angel's performance, I wondered where her parents were. I was reluctant to break the spell of this magical dance, so I did not allow my thoughts to become words. Finally, my mom mode proved stronger than the moment, and I asked, "Where are your mommy and daddy?" She turned, pointing proudly toward the stage, to a man doing a sound check at the microphone. With the mystery solved of where her parents were, my angel continued her performance. After a while, the now-identified daddy of my angel eventually wandered over to introduce himself. Or maybe he thought Kayla and I were too intimate for strangers and wanted to make sure my intentions were honorable. If that was the case, I truly wanted to ease his fears. So before he spoke, I blurted out that I had fallen madly in love with his daughter. It is a wonder he did not think I was crazy. However, he only smiled and nodded as if this was a most common phenomenon with his daughter. Was I not the first to be so captivated and chosen? I rejected the thought.

We chatted some more, and I guess I passed the stranger safety test because my friend's daddy returned to the stage, confidently leaving Kayla and me to walk hand in hand to the ladies' room. Her trust in me had no boundaries. Like good girlfriends do in the bathroom, we shared some lip gloss and a hairbrush after we washed up. As we walked back to the auditorium, my angel-turned-dancer decided that walking was way too boring. She suggested we skip. With only the slightest hesitation on my part, we did just that. When we burst—and I mean burst—through the door, we were laughing louder than the band was playing! Suddenly, Kayla went totally still and quiet. I wondered at the abrupt change in her demeanor. I followed her gaze to the stage. Then I saw what she saw and heard what she heard. It was her daddy. He was singing.

She dropped my hand and ran straight for the stage. As I watched her run from me, the room changed, and I felt transported into a realm of reality that was not of this world. I was completely frozen and could actually feel time slow. The band's music became a background symphony to what seemed an epic movie playing before me. Everything swelled in crescendo as my little angel climbed boldly onto the stage. The camera in my mind's eye zoomed in on her as she collected herself and walked quietly over to her daddy. Regally she stood still beside him, molding her body against his. He never stopped singing. I loved that he did not shoo her away or give her a stern don't-do-that parental look. Instead, he put his arm around her, welcoming her to the stage beside him as if it was her rightful place.

I held my breath, now realizing this evening had a divine purpose, and it was about to be revealed. Without missing a note, my angel's daddy bent down and handed her a microphone. She acted as if she expected him to do just that as if she were waiting on it. With the poise of a professional, she began to sing. Angelic was the only word for the sound. Though tiny in stature, she was the only star on stage. She sang without one ounce of self-consciousness, and I longed for things I had no words to express. She sang of her Creator's love, and it surrounded me.

For the second time that night, I felt joy in its purest form.

Overwhelmed, a tear slipped down my cheek, and the joy I felt morphed into a profound sadness. An urgent prayer erupted unexpectedly from my soul. "Protect her! Do not let this world or some circumstance or cruel words steal her essence from her. Right now, she is her truest self!" As I watched her, it became obvious to me that she was well-loved. She was so well loved that it had birthed a confidence in her that enabled her to hug strangers, dance with abandon, and sing from a stage. She knew her role in this world—to love and be loved. "Lord, please don't let her lose that," I continued to pray. "Please don't let anyone steal that from her." As I prayed, I felt no assurance, no divine certainty that my prayer would be answered.

During my prayer, my angel finished her song and was lifted into her daddy's safe arms. He sang, holding his daughter. As he continued, she put her head on his shoulder, and her eyes grew so heavy that they finally closed. The now-sleeping angel, dancer, and star of the show rested her precious head on her daddy's shoulder, tired from just being her. More tears flowed down my cheeks. I cried for what would be lost in her future and for what had been lost in my past.

She is you, and you were her.

These words were in me and around me. I heard them in my spirit. I was in a lonely silence when they poured into my heart. The revelation did not shock me. In that moment, there was no truer truth.

It sounds strange to say it aloud, but right then, I fell in love with me—the me I used to be a long, long time ago. Another prayer erupted from my soul, but this one was all for me:

> I want her back. I want to be *that* me. It was once the most natural thing in the world to live like a well-loved child, hearing the sound of your voice and loving the sound of my own. However, as I grew older, the whispers of *stranger, stranger, danger, danger* grew louder and caused me to hide my heart. Before I realized it, I stopped hugging strangers. I stopped dancing with abandon, and I gave up the starring role of my own life. I stopped being me—on purpose. I exchanged that role for that of an understudy in other people's lives. I guess I hoped to share their applause, never believing I would have any of my own. Please forgive me for believing that the audience of many could replace You as my audience of One. Forgive me for loving cautiously instead of extravagantly.

Forgive me for protecting my heart rather than sharing it.

Forgive me for not being me, the me You created me to be.

A stillness and quiet peace overcame my soul when I finished my words.

The band ended their song as I ended my prayer, and I was transported back to the real world. At the same time, my little angel opened her eyes and saw me across the room. As our eyes locked, I was infused with hope—for her and me. She quickly left her daddy's arms and ran, jumping into mine. "Can I go home with you?" she asked me very seriously. I laughed, hugging her tight, and this time I did not hesitate. Together we danced to the last of the music. I felt much younger than I had in a very long time.

My Creator used this little angel as another clue, a signpost directing me toward me and my destiny. *You just get to be you.* God used an unexpected encounter with an angel to remind me of that.

Our Creator constantly invades our ordinary, attempting to woo us to the extraordinary. Distractions, discouragement, and disappointment blind us to who we are and what we are supposed to be doing. My journey of uncovering my identity and discovering my destiny helped me clarify and crystallize who I am and what I am supposed to be doing. What I discovered was so simple. What I was supposed to be doing was just being me—confidently—just as I had been when I was a child and just like my angel friend, Kayla. I thank my Creator for the introduction. She is now a part of my story.

Your life is writing a story—your story—where you are the main character and the star! Like all good stories, there are times of intense struggle, glorious adventure, pitifully ordinary days, and seasons of pain. However, when we view our lives through the lens of time, we can begin to see a common thread being woven throughout the years of our life. With the busyness and distractions of life, however, that thread is very easy to miss. I almost missed mine.

Max Lucado has been a big help in my journey of purpose. I do not know Max personally, but I feel like I do because I have read all of his books. He is such a great storyteller. His book *Cure for the Common Life: Living in Your Sweet Spot* was another instrument my Creator used to lead me into my destiny. There is a fabulous assessment in it called S.T.O.R.Y. In it, you are asked to write down very specific memories—one from childhood, one from your teen years, and one from your adult memory—when you were completely and utterly yourself. Not just happy memories but significant moments when you were simply and completely being you. Max encourages you to try to look back through the years as an observer instead of a participant in your own story. Consult your Creator to bring out the very memory that reflects the true essence of you. This exercise requires some time and prayer. Do not be discouraged if nothing comes to you immediately—keep consulting your Creator. Also, buy the book.

When you have remembered your moment, write a one-line summary of it, the details of how you did it, and then describe what was most satisfying to you. This experience could have occurred in ten minutes, a day, a week, a summer, or even a year. This experience could have come from any part of your life—school, work, church, play yard, neighborhood, home, extracurricular activities, volunteering experience, travel, or any segment of your life.

Here are the guidelines outlined in Max's book that are helpful when thinking about your moment:[15]

- It must be important to you, though it doesn't matter what anyone else thinks of it.

- It must be a specific event or experience, not a general activity or feeling.

- It must be a specific accomplishment to you, but not a milestone such as a birthday.

- It must be specific in actions. For example, "I was good at . . ." or "I succeeded at . . ." not "I loved to play the piano" or "I loved to play softball."

When I did this exercise, I was sitting in the hospital waiting room as my husband was being taken into surgery for his injured golf elbow (sometimes our passions can land us in the hospital). As I was waiting, I was reading and thinking of memories when I was just being me. The childhood memory that first popped into my mind made me smile. It was one I had not thought about in years. It reminded me of Kayla. My first time being in a play, my first time on a stage. I was a vegetable—like a literal carrot. I was five years old and loved every minute of being on stage so much that I was in a play every year afterward until I stopped being me. It did not matter if I was a pilgrim or an Indian, a farmer or a cow, a tree or a flower—I played each part like opening night on Broadway!

No one had to encourage me to practice my lines. I would stand in front of a mirror for hours, perfecting my performance. When I was little, I loved to watch myself in a mirror. Neither mirrors nor a stage frightened me at that age. A few years into my young acting career, the annual productions were not frequent enough to fulfill my need to perform in front of an audience, so I started writing and producing my own plays. Not only did I write the plays and produce them, but I also gave myself the starring role. I found the costumes for the other actors, who usually included my brother, sister, and all the neighborhood children—

the McLeods were my go-to family. I assigned them their parts. I helped them rehearse their lines. I cheered them on. I advertised the event, sold tickets for the event, and shamelessly knocked on doors inviting everyone I knew and anyone I did not know to come see me perform. My favorite part was seeing people come together in one place at one time for something I had a passion for—telling the story. I believed I could tell it better than anyone else could. It was all so very natural to me. I laughed at the little girl I once was. She was bossy. I recorded this memory in my journal.

The next memory that came to mind, and again one I had not thought of in years, was when I was a sophomore in high school. I was leading a triple life. I had a church life, a home life, and my life as a teenager in high school. All were very different identities. I was trying so hard to be who everyone wanted me to be. It was exhausting. Looking for relief, I decided to go on our summer youth trip with my church. The location was out in my beloved wide-open spaces. I can remember lots of trees and a huge lake. I do not remember much else. I do not remember the activities we participated in, the songs we sang, or the speakers we heard, but I do remember giving up. I remember asking for and receiving forgiveness for not being me. It was a physical experience. I literally felt a heavy weight lift off my body. I felt like a new person. And I felt like me for the first time in a long time. I wanted to tell everyone I knew, to shout the news from the rooftops or a stage. I got my chance. Our youth group leader asked me to share my experience—from a stage. I had not been on one once since I quit doing plays and being me. I was scared to death and yet so excited. Just as I had done when I was a little girl, I called everyone I knew and even some that I did not, asking them to come see me and hear my story. My three lives were about to be in the same room. I was about to take off my mask and unveil me. The urgency I felt was overwhelming. I wanted everyone to experience what I had, though I was not even sure what to call my experience. I felt my Creator so strongly urging me on, giving me confidence. That night came, and the room was filled. Everyone I invited had come, or so it seemed. My parents were front and center. My friends as well. I took the stage. Fearless. I had no notes. I spoke my heart, and people responded. I got it. For a moment during my teenage years, I dared to be me, and I impacted others. I had tangible evidence that me being me mattered. Sadly, I remembered, it did not last for long. I could not hold on to her, and I went back to being what others either wanted or needed me to be. As I wrote down this memory in my journal, sadness enveloped me in that hospital waiting room as I recorded all my regrets.

For my adult story, many came to mind. In my twenties, I was the person you called to find out which bar had been designated the "happy hour" location. My nickname was "Social Director" at Southern Farm Bureau. In my thirties,

I planned fundraisers for my son Austin's football team and introduced and organized Southern supper clubs in our California neighborhood. I was the fundraising director for the PTA of my younger sons' school and planned elegant galas that raised a lot of money. For six months, I trained, led, and encouraged a group of thirty-five women to hike sixteen miles in Yosemite National Park and climb the infamous cables leading to the top of Half Dome. Again, I called everyone I knew. I assigned teams and roles. I planned for months. Cresting that summit with those women was a powerful experience. However, to date, as I sat in the hospital waiting room, the greatest adult memory I had of me just being me was planning the first Courage Conference. I felt like a little girl again. I imagined the stage from where I would speak and the colors of the decorations. I shared the dream of the conference and built a team from a group of women I loved. I wrote the lines and planned the songs. I designed posters and advertised the event in our small community. I worked on the flowers and the seating chart. I invited everyone I knew to join me . . . and they did! When I took that stage and said aloud for the first time, *"You were created on purpose for a purpose. Do you have the courage to be you?"* I felt as if I were in a bubble where there was no time. It was all effortless. I was being me, and it was so easy. It was the moment I longed for, the one I vowed would last a lifetime.

When I did this exercise, I almost fell out of my chair.

Thank you, Max, for helping me connect the dots of my story. What I discovered was truly a profound "a-ha" moment in my life. I almost yelled aloud to all the weary family members in the surgery waiting room with me the truth that seared into my soul!

Drumroll, please!

I love to bring people together for a purpose. I have been doing it all my life in some shape, form, or fashion.

Whatever I am doing, whatever I am passionate about (which has certainly changed throughout my life), whatever propels me into action—I want everyone I know and a multitude of people I do not to come and do it with me! I do not like parties that much because typically there is no purpose. I do not like games for the same reason. I would rather we all *do* something that has meaning. I do not like to take girls' trips or just hang out unless there is a task to accomplish. I could not see the contradiction before.

I love people, but I am task-oriented and driven. My heart and my passion are for people to come together for a common purpose to change the world! This is what I recorded in my journal—just in time because they were wheeling my husband out of surgery.

This nugget of truth was in every example and story I wrote. As I reviewed the words in my journal, I realized I had not always been doing it for the right purposes. Happy Hour organization was not world-changing. This exercise was a tremendous clue as to who I was and what I loved to do—what I was created to do and what was natural for me. It confirmed I was not a random cosmic accident. This discovery shouted that I had been created on purpose for a purpose in such a tangible way! I was stirred up—body, soul, and spirit. For years, I used my passion for my purposes, but now I sensed it was for something greater than my own. *For what?* I wondered. I consulted my Creator.

"What are Your plans for this planet that I am uniquely created for?" I asked.

It felt like the right question. No longer was this journey about me and what I wanted. I sensed there was something unique for me to do that only I could do with a purpose much greater than I dared to ask or imagine. Revelation dawned. When we unite our purposes with our Creator's purposes, the supernatural is engaged. When we quit trying to be who we want to be and do all we want to do, then miracles begin to happen. The power deposited within us is ignited, and the angels in heaven are dispatched to our aid! Now I was zip-lining. Adrenaline coursed through me. I had such a sense of urgency to be and do all I was created to. The clues were mounting up. I was ready. I could feel and almost taste my thing to do—my water-walking, giant-slaying, history-making destiny was just around the corner.

What about you? Any "a-ha" moments? Connecting any dots?

Seeds of desire were planted deep within each of us long before time began. From the moment we arrive on this planet, it seems there is a war to bury or kill off those dreams and desires. That is why we need courage. That is why our Creator provides us with clues. They are in my story, and they are in your story. They are in the places and times you were just being you. Remember, consult your Creator.

You can be all you were created to be and do all you were created to do if you actively pursue you!

My prayer for you today is that you will rest in that knowledge. Clues are coming. You have not messed anything up. We all have regrets when we look back over our lives. Do not focus on what was lost or what you did not do. Focus on the moments when you were just being you. Your Creator has not given up on you, and neither have I. Release your worries. Daily seek your Creator and look for clues.

CHAPTER 19

What Breaks Your Heart?

*T*he year 2000 was the year when I began asking the life-altering questions *Who am I?* and *What am I supposed to be doing?* That year, I decided to pick a word to live by and focus on instead of making the typical New Year's resolutions that I never seem to succeed at anyway. Resolutions seemed to me to be an exercise in failure that only proved my severe lack of willpower and self-control. Thus my life-altering decision to focus on a single word for the entire year.

I chose the word *intentional* for the millennium year 2000. It was my fortieth birthday year. I decided I wanted to live the next forty years differently from the last. I was determined to learn to live life intentionally instead of frantically in reaction mode. Having a word to focus on helped me do just that. I decided to become extremely focused and intentional about three things that year. The first was to intentionally tell the people in my life how much I love and appreciate them. I had a haunting dream that one day I would go to the funeral of someone I loved madly and be draped over a casket sobbing uncontrollably,

"I wish I had told them _____."

I never wanted to have to fill in that blank. I just wanted the people I loved to know they mattered to me and how I felt about them. I took courage and started being intentional.

My second intentional decision and focus was to daily seek my Creator—the God I had believed in my entire life—to tell me who I was and what I was supposed to be doing. Third, I wanted to be intentional in living my life on purpose for a purpose—a purpose bigger than myself. Those simple decisions and focus drastically changed my life, and I know they will change yours.

I had so much fun, and I loved my word for the year 2000 so much that I adopted the practice for each year thereafter. No longer was I a failure at resolutions; instead, I was a success in focus and intentionality, so much so that the people in my life began to notice.

In the second year, 2001, I chose the words *prayer-filled*. That meant slowing down, becoming thoughtful, and deciding to pray about everything before reacting. It was the year I learned what it meant to have conversations with my Creator. The next year, *aware* was my word of focus, and on and on it went. Each year, around September or October, I consult my Creator about a new word, a new focus, or a lesson to learn for the coming year. *Anticipation, abandon, power,* and *able* were a few I focused on. *Foundations, move forward, breakthrough,* and *harvest* were more I felt. Each word focused my days for the year and provided many lessons along the way, and some even came with divine promises, but none more than my word for the year 2011.

Fulfillment.

Ah, that word, at that specific time, was music to my parched soul. I had been pregnant with dreams that felt impossible for so long—for years—and yet I chose to believe. I was even making a bit of progress. Clues were being provided as we settled into our life, making our home in Sacramento. I continued speaking my dreams and beliefs aloud and in a dramatic fashion, and there were those who stood with me and believed. But on most days, Jake was the only one who listened. However, when I chose this word, or rather, when this word was divinely chosen for me, I believed it meant things were about to change. This whispered word meant my dreams, desires, and destiny were about to be revealed and fulfilled.

It was the fall of 2010. My husband had been diagnosed with cancer, and we were waiting for the surgery to be scheduled. I received the diagnosis and my word around the same time. *Fulfillment* did not seem to fit with the diagnosis. However, over the past eleven years, my Creator taught me that my dreams and destiny often would not line up with my circumstances. I had evidence. His Word and His promises were something I could cling to and trust in the midst of a storm. So I did. I clung to peace instead of worry—trust instead of stress. Suddenly my hectic life and busy calendar were completely cleared as we waited for results from biopsies and surgeries. I sensed in my spirit that I was to take this time to rest and remember. It was a very strong sense I attributed to my Creator. I read a devotion that said,

> *Be careful to remember all your eyes have seen, do not let them slip through your heart, teach them to your children and to your children after them . . . remember the day it all changed.*

Thank God my husband's surgery removed all the cancer! Through my gratitude, I kept the challenge to remember and write down "all my eyes have seen."

Three years prior, on July 22, 2007, all my questions about purpose and destiny were revealed while my heart was shattered into a million pieces. Fulfillment would come four years later.

It's a Home

It's a home. It's a home. It's a home. Those words were whispered to my heart one Sunday morning as I sat in church as I had for most every Sunday morning of my entire life. Being raised in Mississippi, the Bible Belt, this habit was established early in my life, but in all those years of church attendance, never once did I walk through those doors expecting my life to change. However, on Sunday, July 22, 2007, my life did just that.

I sat in the huge auditorium, waiting for the service to begin, engulfed by three thousand people. I did not know a single one of them aside from my two teenage sons who sat beside me. My husband was playing golf, and I was feeling lonely and melancholy that particular day. We had been in Sacramento for a year, fighting to survive. We had lost our home, and we missed our friends and the comfortable life we had built. Hanging on to my identity and destiny during this time was extremely difficult. However, I took courage and chose to believe— daily, in spite of my feelings and circumstances. The whispered words of my Creator kept me going. *"Don't reduce the size of your dreams and desires to accommodate your present circumstances. They won't fit."* Daily, I vowed to try.

Thank God I did try because on that day, everything suddenly changed, everything suddenly made sense, and I knew what I was supposed to do.

It's a home.

There was a guest speaker at church that Sunday morning, Don Brewster. Although a preacher, he did not preach. Instead, he told of how his own heart was broken and recalibrated by God over an issue I had never heard about: sex trafficking.

With his words, he painted a picture I did not want to see. I lived in a world where children are sold for sex.

He told of children in Cambodia, as young as five years old, who were systematically sold to men for sex, sold as if they were a commodity with no value, no feelings or purpose. My body was literally racked with sobs, much to my sons' embarrassment. At one point, I looked around the room to see if I was the only one pierced by the images created in my mind's eye. Everyone looked so normal. I felt I was the only one of the thousands attending that day who could hear these children's cries, feel the trauma they endured, and see the pain in their eyes.

I could feel my heart breaking, violently ripping inside of me. I doubted I would ever be the same.

It's a home. I continued to hear this whispered to my spirit as Don began to tell how his own life had changed when he learned of the plight of these Cambodian children. When he and his wife, Bridget, learned of this hideous crime against children from a TV show they watched, they knew they had to do something. So they did what any of us would do with the same knowledge (*not*, as my teenagers would say). They quit their jobs, sold everything they owned, and moved to Cambodia to start a home for children rescued from the sex slave trade—all with no idea how to do that. He made it sound so simple.

It's a home. At this point in the service, the atmosphere dramatically changed. Instead of horror being recounted over and over, there was hope being delivered in large doses. Don began to tell stories of what a difference a home and a family make in the lives of these vulnerable yet invisible children. He read stories of children who had the privilege of living there, girls who had names and beautiful faces, and who I knew had unique destinies.

It's a home. I wrote those words over and over on my church bulletin. The stories Don told of tangible restoration, the stories of hope and transformation, were ones I believed God was writing, and they caused a seismic shift inside of me. I wanted to be a part of that restoration story. I wanted to bring people together for that purpose. I wanted to shout out loud that these children were created on purpose for a purpose. I could hardly remain silent. The stories Don told reminded me of the ones I had heard as a small child going to church on Sunday. It was the story of God doing extraordinary things through ordinary people. Don said he was one. I wanted to be another. I realized it was a story our Creator wanted to write on each of our lives . . . including the lives of these vulnerable children.

It's a home.

For days after that church service, I prayed, "Cambodia? You want me to go to Cambodia?" I really did not think my husband, in our current financial and emotional situation, was going to agree to move our family to Cambodia. In fact, I was certain of it. So instead, I wrote the biggest donation check that would clear our bank account to the Brewster's nonprofit organization, thinking that would satisfy the ache in my heart and maybe even the prompting of my Creator. It did not work. I still cried for weeks. I literally cried for all the children around the world being sold to strangers by the parents who were supposed to love and protect them. I cried as if they were my own daughters. When I confided to a friend that I thought I was going crazy with grief for children I had never met who felt like my own, she told me that she believed God was letting me feel His heart for these precious little ones. "It's unbearable," I sobbed.

Eventually, I fought with my Creator over this hideous issue of selling children for sex. "You could make this stop. You could take it off the table. Make this issue, the issue of selling children, cease!" I angrily demanded.

I felt a whispered response in my heart: *What age would that be? Five years old? Ten? Is it okay for a fifteen-year-old to be tortured, raped, and sold for sex? A twenty-five-year-old?* I could see this argument with my Maker was going nowhere, so I shouted from the depths of my soul, "JUST DO SOMETHING!" And before I had time to take a breath, He said to me, *Why don't you?*

That was a holy moment.

Time stood still.

It's a home.

"I'm just a mom," I whined.

Good, because that is just what they need—a mom, a family. These are your daughters, the daughters you have longed for. Find them, build them a home, and call them family.

I gasped. These were my daughters! Everything became clear. My dreams were about to be fulfilled. Courage House: it's a home for children rescued from sex trafficking.

Do Something!

As the weeks and months of 2007 came and went, I continued to be broken-hearted for children I had never met but who felt like my own. Though I battled daily through our family's difficult financial situation, the desire to *do something* for these kids did not diminish but accelerated in my spirit. During the beginning of 2008, I sought direction, answers, and wisdom from the place all God-fearing people go . . . Google. I began researching the words "sex trafficking" and "human trafficking," expecting to see details of this horrific crime in faraway countries I had never visited. I was shocked to the core of my being when the words appeared on my screen: "Sacramento."

Sacramento? My home? My city? Through my research, I learned children were being sold for sex right in my own backyard—in my city, my state, and in my country! While the reality of children being sold in Cambodia broke my heart, the news that they were being sold in my own backyard outraged me and propelled me into action! This time I did not have to take courage; I was angry and bold.

Anger was my fuel and energy.

I remembered the Enneagram assessment I had taken back in the early years of my identity boot camp, and anger had been identified as a facet of my personality. I remembered being confused because I really did not get angry with much. However, as I made a careful assessment of who I was, I learned my Maker had deposited anger inside me when I encountered injustices that required change. Up until that point in my life, I just had not encountered much that you would call injustice.

Now I got it. At that moment, I believed with everything I was that I had been created on purpose *for this purpose* because I was totally confident in my identity. I knew rescuing these children, my daughters, was my destiny.

Everything made sense. My life was at the pivotal point of convergence—when everything in your life lines up. When every experience, every job, every conversation, every assessment, and even every struggle makes sense. I knew what I had to do. But even more exciting, I knew what I was created to do. I had been divinely equipped for it my entire life. My journey of purpose during the last seven years served to show me how. I am a mom—a nurturer. I am a cheerleader—an encourager. I am a conduit—a leader to gather people for a passionate purpose. I am a communicator—a loud voice angry at injustice. I am an activist—I have to do something. Though still extremely ordinary, I am a water walker, giant slayer, and history maker.

These invisible children were my long-awaited daughters, and my purpose at this point in my life was to build them a home and call them family. My life and my journey led me to this moment. I felt like I was standing on the ledge of an airplane, and someone was screaming, *"JUMP!"*

So I did.

"We are going to build a Courage House in every city around the world that needs one . . . starting with my city, Sacramento, California."

It's a home.

It sounded so simple and, at the same time, impossible. Yet I felt compelled to say it aloud.

I had already started Courage to Be You, Inc., before I left the Bay Area. We thought we would be producing Courage Conferences and encouraging individuals around the world to uncover their identities and discover their destinies. I believed the children I had heard about needed to do just that. I just had no idea how to bring it about.

When I eventually met Bridget Brewster, Pastor Don's wife, I asked her, "How? What do you do? How do you start?"

She gave me the perfect answer: one step at a time.

So that was what I did. I picked up the phone and courageously called a woman who worked at the state capitol in California and who had authored a state-funded report regarding human trafficking in our state. I asked if it were true. She said yes. All throughout the report I read, it stated there was a lack of services for victims and that restoration homes were needed. I told her I would build one. Imagine my surprise when she invited me to a meeting at the capitol!

Now I needed courage.

The state capitol? The fear of embarrassment raised its ugly head, but I squashed it with words of belief. I may have been scared to death, but I was walking on water. I did not have any money, much less a college degree or a staff, but I had a vision and the knowledge (finally) of what I was on this planet to do. However, I had to stop looking at the waves crashing up around my ankles, or I would sink—fast. So I took my friend Terry's advice and remembered that I was a child of God and started acting like it. I dressed in my best, most professional outfit, did my hair and makeup, and then got in my car and drove downtown for my first meeting at the state capitol. I truly felt like a country bumpkin coming to town, accompanied by my Southern accent still intact after fifteen years in California.

As I drove, I made a deal with my Creator. I would go to that meeting, but I was not going to say a word! I was going to be quiet because I did not want to look as stupid as I felt. These were the experts; I was a novice. I knew my place, but I must have forgotten who I was. (Me, be quiet?) Still, I tried. For two hours I listened as experts, professionals, and government officials talked about the enormous problem of human trafficking and child sex trafficking in our nation and in our state. It seemed like everyone was very familiar with the problem. And they even knew the solution. It's a home. However, no one seemed able to make a decision or authorize the funding and building of one. I could not stand it any longer. Without a conscious thought, I jumped up in the middle of that room, interrupted the conversation, and confidently told them that I was going to build a home for these children—me and my nonprofit organization, Courage to Be You, Inc. (They had no idea I was the only volunteer at the time.) Not satisfied, I went on to say that, in fact, God's people in this city were going to build the home because it was our responsibility. (They had no idea that I knew no one in this town.) I went on and explained that once these good people knew children were being sold for sex, the money would coming pouring in, and we would have plenty of beds for children in need. Then I sat down wondering where that boldness and those words came from.

No one said a word. They did not even look at me. They just began talking again about the problem as if I had not said a word.

When the meeting ended, I ran to my car in my high heels. I cried all the way home. I felt like the village idiot. Yes, I had forgotten that crazy was a part of this journey. I felt sorry for myself and did not tell anyone about this experience. However, I was getting madder. I screamed at my Maker, "What was that?" Silence.

That was February 2008. Haunted by the idea of my daughters being raped, abused, and tortured night after night, I finally got over myself, and when I saw an article in the newspaper about the issue, I summoned the courage to pick up the phone to call the Sacramento Police Department. Once again, I was walking on water, trying to keep from sinking. I dialed the number and asked for the department that dealt with crimes against children. I was told to hold. I had a strong urge to hang up.

But before I did, Detective Haun introduced himself. Detective? He sounded way above my pay grade.

With all the courage I could muster, and in my most professional voice, I said, "My name is Jenny Williamson, and my nonprofit, Courage to Be You, is building homes for minor victims of sex trafficking around the world. Do you think the Sacramento area is in need of one?" (I sounded crazy to myself!) However, this stranger did not seem to think so. He took me dead seriously, asked if I would like to meet an officer who was working directly with these young victims, and then replied, "Thank you. We need that home. How soon can you build it?" I had no answer, which with water-walking, giant-slaying, history-making destinies, you do not have to have one. Whew.

He gave me the officer's name and phone number. I called her and arranged to meet her for coffee. Officer Pam, I called her. I shared my dream of Courage House, a home for these young victims, and she told me about the kids she was attempting to recover. She said there were those who called them throwaways. With tears in her eyes, she said to me, "I often wonder who these kids were supposed to have been." Ah! She got it. They *were* created on purpose for a purpose. I was heartbroken all over again and getting madder by the minute. With no safe place to go when rescued, Officer Pam had taken them into her home and was using her own money to buy them food and clothes. (Shhh, don't tell anyone—we do not want to get her in trouble.) As we talked, she confirmed, "We need a home. They are going to die in this life." She did not think I was crazy; instead, she asked if I would like to meet the FBI Innocence Lost Task Force leader, who had a mandate from the federal government to rescue these vulnerable children and put away their perpetrators. I did not hesitate—my answer was yes. I arranged another coffee meeting to meet FBI Special Agent Minerva. I wondered at her name. It sounded like someone's old aunt. When she walked through the doors of our coffee shop, she was anything but old. When I learned the meaning of her name, it all made sense: "goddess of war." She was fighting to rescue these kids.

When I told her the dream of Courage House, not only did she believe me, but she agreed to go around town speaking with me, telling others of this crime against our children. To understand these children and their unique needs, I started hanging out with vice cops and FBI agents. I learned all I could about this vulnerable population. The more I learned, the more my heart broke for them. I made more phone calls to social workers, probation officers, and juvenile justice judges because I learned that most of the kids being rescued were runaways and/or in the foster care system. Many of them were hurt by the people who were supposed to protect them. Did I mention I was getting madder?

Finally, I got the courage to email Pastor Don and Bridget Brewster, asking them how they had built a home for children rescued from sex trafficking in Cambodia, and hoping they would have some kind of a blueprint I could follow because I actually had no idea what I was doing and how I was going to do it. In the meantime, I continued to have coffee with complete strangers, shouting to anyone who would listen that my organization would build Courage House, a home for these children. Then I told the Brewsters via email that I wanted to do in Sacramento what they had done in Cambodia. To my utter delight, they agreed to meet with me. Their yes was such a great encouragement. I shudder to think what would have happened if they were too busy to meet with me.

I met them at our church, where the local newspaper was interviewing them. When Bridget saw me, she grabbed the reporter and photographer and ran over to me. As she approached me, I could hear her enthusiastically telling them, "This is Jenny Williamson, and she is going to do what we have done in Cambodia—build a home for children rescued from sex trafficking right here in Sacramento!" I almost fell on the floor! I was speechless as the reporter asked to interview me, and the photographer took pictures of me. All I could think about was how I had not told my husband yet!

This was such a crazy time in my life. Things were happening so fast that I could not keep up. Amid all that was happening with regard to sex trafficking, a friend of mine had moved to Africa to work at an orphanage there. She told me that there was so much land and they just needed someone to come plant a garden. I volunteered my dad without him knowing it. He said yes and started to walk on water at sixty-nine years of age. This trip was the first of many to Africa to plant gardens, build churches, and feed widows and orphans. My mom joined him. A year later, I was invited to join them in Tanzania, Africa, to produce and speak at a Courage Conference. I finally had a passport. My little-girl dream of traveling the world to tell people of their loving Creator was about to be fulfilled. While I was there, I was given a building out in the bush. I wondered what I needed with a building in Africa. I did not have much time to ponder the thought because when my plane touched back down in Sacramento, there was another article in the newspaper on child sex trafficking.

My meetings were increasing, and I was running around town like a chicken with my head cut off, passionately telling strangers in coffee shops about the needs of these vulnerable victims. I was drinking so much coffee that I was beginning to think I could fly. Finally, I invited everyone who had expressed a desire to see this home built into one room with decision-makers to formally and publicly announce that we would build this home. I invited the Brewsters to speak about the difference the home in Cambodia had made to children there. I asked the local police department and FBI task force to detail for this group of community leaders the incredible number of young children who were being sold in our city. To my utter amazement, sixty people showed up. Judges, lawyers, child welfare workers, probation officers, lawmakers, and many others, including the local newspaper. I again declared that we were going to build a home for children who have been trafficked for sex. The reporter again took my picture and asked me for my office number. Since I did not have one, I gave her my home phone.

The next morning our phone began to ring at 5:00 a.m. The reporter printed a full-page article in the *Sacramento Bee* about the issue of trafficking and my dream to build a home. There was my picture and home photo plastered across the *Sacramento Bee*. Over two hundred people called or emailed me on that day, starting at 5:00 a.m., much to my husband's surprise, saying, "We want to help build the home."

These two hundred people, who on that day decided to read the newspaper and were moved by their Maker to call or email me, were the answer to the prayers I had been praying to my Creator: *How? When? Who? Where are your people?*

With that one newspaper article, He sent me an army!

He also sent me something else—evidence that this home was needed.

Of those two hundred phone calls, I received three from women who identified themselves as prostitutes—their word, not mine. I was so shocked that each of them said the very same thing to me: "Please build the home. It is too late for me, but if there had been a place when I was a teen on the streets, maybe my life would be different. Please build this home. All they need is someone to believe in them."

Over and over, I began to hear the words, *Believe in me, believe in me. Who would I be if you believed in me?*

It was as if I could hear the voices of the children crying out in the night. My heart was literally breaking, and I believed I heard my Creator whisper, *Who would they be if they believed in Me?*

Passion, purpose, and urgency filled my spirit! These homes must be built, these children must be rescued. They just need a family and someone to believe in them.

On the same day of the newspaper article and subsequent phone calls, Officer Pam called me and wanted me to meet her for lunch. She had a sixteen-year-old who had been repeatedly trafficked for sex and wanted to introduce me to this young girl she had befriended. I immediately said no. I had purposefully avoided this very thing. How could I look into the eyes of a child who had been tortured in this way and just say, "Hang on, I'm praying for you. I have a dream to build a home, but I have no idea how it will happen"?

"No, thank you," I said. However, police officers can be very persuasive—and they carry guns. So I went to the Chevy's on the river to meet this child. I was so nervous. She looked like any teenager I had met. She could have been a friend of my sons. She knew I knew her story. Prompted by my cop friend, I told her mine and the dream of Courage House. She listened, and I had no idea what she was thinking. I asked if there were such a place, would she come. Without looking me in the eye, she just nodded her head. I tried to engage her in conversation, so I asked what these girls would need most at Courage House. When I paused for her answer, she was staring at her uneaten food. Then without hesitation, she looked into my eyes and said, "They just need someone to believe in them."

Believe in me, believe in me. Who would I be if you believed in me?

I tried to answer all the phones calls and emails I received on that day. It took weeks, and all during that time I continued to be haunted by the words *believe in me.*

One afternoon as I was waiting for one of my coffee dates, I was writing the words on paper and whispered a prayer, *Are these words a song?* Inspiration flooded my soul. We need a song, a video to tell the story of these children. Their stories were so horrific that it was difficult to find the words to explain. *Yes, a song, that is what we need.* Then I laughed because I cannot carry a tune in a bucket, much less write a song. I wondered who would write this song and film this video. Maybe it would be someone else's destiny.

My coffee date that day was Stephanie Midthun, a woman whose husband pastored a local church and who would become my battle buddy in this fight. As she sat down, she saw my scribbled words on a piece of scratch paper.

"What's that?" she inquired.

"A song," I laughed and told her the story.

She smiled confidently. "I'm a songwriter." Of course, she was. She went on to tell me how she had raised tens of thousands of dollars for an orphanage in Africa. Africa, hmm. I told her I had just been given a building there.

I ripped the paper from my notebook and asked her to write a song called "Believe in Me." She agreed. Days later, I cried as I read the lyrics, and in January 2009 on National Anti-Human Trafficking Day, I had the privilege to hear Christina Smit, a fifteen-year-old, sing the words written by Stephanie, inspired by three women who had no hope for their own home but who longed for someone to *believe in me.*

That song, and later a phenomenal music video also titled "Believe in Me," written and produced by a young filmmaker, Aaron Schnobrich, who volunteered all his time for the project, became the vehicle our organization used to tell the story of children who were being raped, abused, tortured, and sold for sex in our very own backyard. The newspaper article brought a team, an army of people, to the organization, Courage to Be You, Inc., and we all vowed to build the home. All our hearts were broken over these young ones. We began to challenge people to do what they loved to do for these children, and they did. We were especially blessed by the local music community and bands like The Reel, The Music Room, and performing artist Chaya, who donated songs and helped produce a music CD to raise funds for the home. We then began doing Courage Concerts to be a voice for these voiceless children. People responded.

As I write these words to you, my heart begins to pound. It was such a special time in my life. I had gone from being alone with my dreams to now daily working with an incredible volunteer team. Not one person received a dime in pay. We were all volunteers and vowed not to take a cent for ourselves until that home was built. Our faith was the fuel. At the time, we all thought we were a little crazy and out on the proverbial limb. However, we were walking on water and loving every minute of it. We all had the courage to be who we were created to be and encouraged everyone we met to do the same.

When I came to understand my Creator wanted me to build this home, I kept asking all the logical logistical questions like, *Where? When? How?* When I got no answer or sense of direction, I decided to wait and just believe it would all be brought to me in time. I figured anyone could hire a realtor, find land, and engage a banker to finance it.

Soon there was a choir of voices asking the same questions. "Where are you looking for property?" they would ask.

My response would be, "I'm not looking."

"Have you hired a realtor?"

"No," was my response. I wanted a story to wow the world. I wanted to be an example of how God uses ordinary people to do extraordinary things. So I waited, believing my Creator wanted to do the impossible for these vulnerable, abused children. He wanted to do it through me and the small team of individuals that made up Courage to Be You, Inc., now called Courage Worldwide.

One year later, I received the address to Courage House.

I was standing on a stage at a Courage Conference, encouraging the crowd to dream big impossible dreams by challenging them with the question, *Do you have the courage to be you?* I was also telling them about my pursuit of purpose and how it led me to a group of vulnerable children. "We need fifty acres of land in a rural community far away from downtown. We need wide-open spaces at the base of the mountains. I can hear running water, and I see horses. There is a white picket fence around the property," I boldly declared from the stage.

After the conference was over, a woman walked up to me with tears running down her cheeks and said, "I have your home. It is fifty acres in a rural area. It is at the base of the foothills, and there is a creek that runs right down the middle of the property. There are horses and, yes, there is a white fence around the entire property. And it is for sale."

We both cried. I was not even sure if she was real—maybe she was an angel. I looked for the property that night on the internet when I got home. I wept as the wide-open spaces came into view. It was exactly what I had imagined. To see what I had only dreamed was indescribable. My first thought was, *I'm not crazy*. I went to visit the property the next week, and I knew in my spirit that this was the Promised Land, the address of the first Courage House. This would be the place young girls would come to find healing and restoration. This would be the place where I welcomed my daughters home.

Though it looked impossible, I believed. It was my destiny.

I knew that I was going to have to call on all the lessons I had learned during boot camp. The property cost over $1,100,000, and we only had $10,000 in the bank. I guessed it was time to find a realtor as crazy as I was! My Creator was once again asking me to trust Him and not play it safe. He was asking me to walk on water, to risk being thought of as crazy.

The realtor found me.

The weekend before we met, I spoke at a small church of about two hundred people in the Lake Tahoe area. I told them we live in a world where children are sold for sex. I told them about the property. I asked them to pray for me. Immediately after the service, they held an emergency board meeting and then handed me a check for $40,000. This was real! I now had $50,000 in the bank for when I made the offer on a $1,100,000 piece of property.

I met the realtor the next day and asked how he felt about making an offer on a piece of property when we only had $50,000 in the bank. He laughed and said, "Sure." Though I was scared to death, I signed the contracts, making an offer on a piece of property I believed would one day be home to children who did not have one. I felt a little crazy.

The offer was refused.

I was shocked. Really, I was. They had taken an offer that included $600,000 as a down payment. I went back to my Creator, trying to determine what just happened. *Fight for it.* So we did. We fought for these children. We continued to hold Courage Concerts and Courage Runs and any other type of fundraiser we could think of to raise the funds to bring these children home. At the same time, a courageous young woman I met agreed by faith to go to Tanzania, Africa, and begin getting the building we had been given there ready to welcome children. We now saw the need for a Courage House there; children were being sold for sex in the area where we had been given a building. Lauren was the young woman's name. She is a true water walker.

I received a phone call from our realtor. "The offer fell through. The owners want to know if you still would like the home and the land."

"Yes!"

"How much money do you have now?"

"Three hundred fifty thousand dollars!" Our events were proving successful, and the community responded generously in the worst economic year since the Great Depression.

We made another crazy offer—no response from the owners. We kept praying and kept raising awareness and funds. The offer expired.

Another four months passed, and the realtor called again. "The owners have another offer on the property and wanted to know if you wanted to make one also."

"Yes!"

"How much money do you have now?"

"Six hundred fifty thousand dollars—still very short of one million."

It was late 2009, almost 2010, and the economic forecast was still dismal for the United States. Many people said our quest was impossible in this climate and that there was no way we could pull this off. They were right—but we believed God could.

We made another offer. We waited, we prayed, and we believed. The results were not ours to produce. We had done our part. We persevered and participated in the process. We were at peace.

The phone rang on February 2, 2010. "The owner will accept your offer and is willing to finance the remainder of the balance for you over the next seven years, with a twenty-five-year amortization. Do you want to accept this offer?"

"Yes! Oh, yes!" I screamed. I sang, I danced, and I called everyone I knew. I wept and sobbed over the miracle I had participated in!

The simple dream became a reality. We had a home. Well, actually, we had two homes. We purchased the fifty acres of land, a house, and a barn for the first U.S.A. Courage House, in a rural area outside of Sacramento, California, and, additionally, we were given horses to begin our equestrian program. We also leased a building for free in Tanzania, Africa, for what was to become the first International Courage House.

We had the homes. Now we needed the girls.

They arrived two months later, one eighteen and one twenty-three. One found me on the internet when she saw the music video "Believe in Me" and emailed me, encouraging me to build the home, all the while believing it was too late for her.

The other stalked me at our concerts and events. She finally confronted me in the bathroom at one venue and said, "I am one of your daughters."

Both called me "mom" without hesitation and, in the most childlike manner, assumed that since they were my daughters that my husband was their dad and my sons their brothers. I laugh and tell everyone that they came for lunch, then for dinner. They came for a weekend and then longer at Thanksgiving. They stayed two weeks at Christmas and a month in February. Somewhere along the way, we called them family.

My Creator fulfilled the dreams and desires He placed in the heart of a child long before time began. I had married a man I loved and birthed sons, had spoken on a stage, was writing a book, was given daughters, and had traveled to a faraway place telling the people there of a Creator who created them on purpose for a purpose. My mom had been right. California was to be my mission field, but it was also the place I would also remember who I was and have the courage to be and do all I was created to. It was the place where my dreams and destiny were fulfilled.

CHAPTER 20

Quitting Isn't an Option

I was walking off a stage in a church in Placerville, California, after giving an emotional talk on the reality of child sex slavery in our country. The pastor followed me to wrap up the evening and ask for an offering. He stood still and silent on the stage. I could feel his emotions and watched as he struggled to control them. Silence enveloped the room, and you could hear people crying. We were all overcome with the images and stories of young girls whose bodies were being ravaged nightly while we slept in our safe homes.

Finally, the pastor looked up and passionately declared, "The church needs to go straight to hell!"

We were all in stunned shock.

"Because that is where these children are—in hell."

He was right. These children, my daughters, are living in hell. These children are not going to come knocking on our doors, asking for help. Someone is going to have to rescue them. Someone is going to have to fight for them, figuratively and literally. I learned that my destiny would require me to be one of those somebodies. It was going to require me to take bold action.

Your destiny is going to require you to do the same. Someone is waiting for you to have the courage to be you. Someone is waiting for you to do something.

My daughter courageously did. Though she was once a victim of this horrendous crime, she did not offer it as an excuse to do nothing. She got her college degree, obtained a teaching certificate, taught her baby sisters at Courage House, and now speaks and trains around the world, helping to set more children free.

If she has to, she will go into enemy territory. Will you? Will you be an agent of change?

We need ordinary men and women who will act boldly.

Simply start by making a careful assessment of who you are. Then you will figure out what you are supposed to be doing. The discovery of your true identity will proceed fulfilling your destiny. Choose to believe you are a child of God—a loving Creator who created you on purpose for a purpose before time began. Choose to believe in spite of your feelings and circumstances. Vow to achieve your water-walking, giant-slaying, history-making destiny.

Yes, you will be scared—but only in the beginning. Begin to anticipate and look forward to the day when you are not afraid anymore. It will come. Something will change. You will be fearless. You will become bold.

The meaning of the word *bold* is to trust, be confident, secure, and sure, to be frank in speech, confident in demeanor, outspoken, blunt, assured, to be free, open and plain, commanding, breaking the silence, acting courageously, daring in all things and in all matters in speaking and acting.

This really is a picture of what it means to live out your destiny.

Boldness comes from making courageous choices over and over again and listening to your Creator, feeling a bit crazy, facing impossible situations, and feeling ordinary but doing the extraordinary. You have been given the honor of participating in the process. You have never felt so alive. You now have something you can live for, but you also have something you would die for.

You are fearless. You are bold. That makes you dangerous. Now there is no way you will ever quit. It is not an option because lives are at stake.

I end this book as I began it—telling you that you have a purpose, an important part to play on this planet. There is something for you to do that only *you* can do. And if you do not do it, it will never get done. Your unique contribution matters—and it will matter to countless people if you quit!

Your destiny may be tied to loving and believing in someone when they cannot love or believe in themselves. *It matters if you quit!* Your destiny may involve consistent and persistent parenting of a child who struggles to learn. *It matters if you quit!* Your destiny may require you to build, write, or create something tangible to share with this world. *It matters if you quit!* Your destiny may be a discovery that literally saves lives, or it may involve giving a hug or writing a note that makes another feel that life is worth living. *It matters if you quit!* Your destiny may be one of persevering in prayer for someone's safety, salvation, or healing. *It matters if you quit!*

You being you matters. Much depends on you having the courage to be you. Quitting is not an option.

> *"I would literally be dead if you had quit or said no.*
> *Thank you for having the courage to be you."*

My adoptive daughters have spoken those words to me numerous times since I met them. Both had pasts that involved extreme sexual abuse and exploitation. Loving them and calling them family felt like the most natural thing in the world to me. It has now been over twenty years since I first heard the words,

> *"Do you have the courage to be you—the you I created?"*

I never contemplated their impact on another person. Now I do. After hearing the story of one of my daughters, now I do. As we come to a close, allow me to share her story (with her permission)—the story of a girl who once called Courage House home:

***

I was born even though my birth mother tried to abort me. From my earliest memories, I knew I was unwanted and that my own mother hated me.

All the adults in my life seemed to hate me, even though I did everything they asked, hoping it would make them love me. But I learned very quickly their love came at a price.

I was taught a religion that was full of rituals accompanied by torment. I went to "church" often and sometimes we even had church at our house. I have seen and experienced things that no one should, especially a child. My birth parents prayed over me and asked that fear and pain be my friends so I would be silent and not talk about the torment and torture.

Until I was twenty-three years old, I never talked without permission.

On my sixth birthday, my birth mother sold me to my uncle with my father's knowledge and consent. I was told, "If you love me, you will do this." So I did.

My uncle told me he owned me, and I believed him. I was owned by something dark and evil that shaped my life for many, many years.

As a child, I was raped, cut, burned, beaten, stabbed, and used in pornography night after night. I was locked in a yellow bedroom that was my own private hell. I never dreamed I would ever leave, but at the same time I silently hoped that a new family would find me and love me.

In the daylight hours, I was let out of my room to go to school and ballet class. I learned to read. My teachers told me I was smart. School became my only escape besides the drugs I was given. Men continued to come in and out of my bedroom at night. Sometimes I fell asleep in class or at the library. It seems strange to me now as an adult that no one ever asked why I was always hungry, tired, bruised, or scared. No one asked why I stopped talking.

I became a child without a voice. Not talking was easier than enduring the punishment of being left alone in the dark for days without food. I thought my life was a mistake and that I was invisible.

At seven, I started traveling to different cities in the U.S. and then to countries around the world with my uncle. He said he wanted me to meet his "friends." Now I was locked in basements and attics where men visited and spoke in languages I didn't understand. I was taught to smile and make them happy or I would have to endure more punishment. We traveled two weeks out of every month. This became my normal.

Every year, the abuse got more hideous and intense. But still I held out hope to be rescued and to find a family who loved me.

When I was fourteen, I met a pastor and his family at a grocery store after school. I was hungry and was contemplating stealing something to eat. This family noticed me and talked with me. They were so kind. They invited me to come on a retreat with them that weekend. I thought I had been saved! I jumped in their minivan aware that this rash decision might get me killed. I went anyway.

The pastor's wife asked me if I needed to call home or get a change of clothes or a toothbrush. I told her that my mom and uncle would never let me go away for the weekend, so either I go with her or I go with them. That was the most I had talked to another human being who wasn't asking me to take my clothes off in a very long time. She stopped asking questions and started driving a little faster.

That weekend I heard words I had never heard before but went straight to my dry heart. I was told I was a wonder, a masterpiece. I was told that I was loved and planned. Though I wanted to believe, I couldn't believe they were meant for me. So I just took advantage of the uninterrupted sleep and the food. I studied the stars and contemplated questions that I thought had no answers.

After the weekend was over, I went back home to my uncle. I decided hope was not for me. Life continued as it always had. By now I believed what I had been told—this was my destiny.

One night, quite unexpectedly, I heard a whisper that wasn't evil—it was around my sixteenth birthday. I believed it was God. He told me that He still calmed storms and He could calm the one inside of me. But I couldn't see the storm ending or if I wanted it to. I decided that responding to the whisper was too risky. Dying felt easier. I literally begged to die. But "they" wouldn't let me.

When I turned eighteen, my life changed dramatically. My uncle died instead of me!

I was free at last! My uncle had left me some money, so I decided to run away and go to college. I knew if I stayed that my family would only sell me again. I was smart and I could read. College made sense. A new life. A new city. I wanted to be somebody different—someone not like me.

But darkness was waiting.

Almost immediately, I met a man who told me I was beautiful. He told me I was special and that he could love me. His words filled up all my empty spaces in my heart, and I believed every word he spoke. He was the very first person I told about my childhood.

And that was the beginning of a new hell that lasted almost four years. My childhood could not compare to life with him. But he told me that my childhood had prepared me well for his plans. He too sold me to any man who would pay his price in cities here in the U.S. and ones around the world. I stopped believing in rescue, in a family, and in good. Now he said I was worthless and that no one would love me. I believed that too and just did what I was told.

But it seems a divine plan was pursuing me.

In September 2009, I saw a video on Facebook called "Believe in Me," produced by Courage Worldwide, showing the life of a young girl being "trafficked" and the vision to build young victims a home, believe in them, and call them family.

I was shocked as I watched. The video was showing my life! The men, the locked doors, the drugs, the torture, and terror. I felt afraid and vulnerable. I didn't know anyone knew. I hated the life I was leading, but seeing it on the screen made me want to run, to leave, to cry, or scream.

But where would I go? I had evidence no one cared about me. But after seeing that video, I just couldn't stay.

That video had such an impact on my life; I decided to send the founder of the organization who produced the video an email. I told Jenny that when I watched that video for the first time, I felt like someone saw me, that someone knew me, and they cared. I told her I had been in an unsafe situation, but now I was going to do something different. I told her that I believed it was too late for me to live in one of her Courage Houses, but I encouraged her to build the homes for other children like me.

I did not think I'd hear back from her. I lived on the East Coast, and she was on the West. I did not tell her in that email that daily I contemplated death, that I had no plan for my life or any idea where to go. Surprisingly, she and a lady in her office emailed me back. They tried to encourage me, but the pull of the past was too strong.

I graduated from college, then I walked back into hell. For two weeks I was surrounded by darkness. Again, I wanted to die, but every time I contemplated it, I would hear the "Believe in Me" song in my head and in my heart.

*Believe in me, believe in me . . . I am longing
for my captive heart to be free.*

It was the longing of my heart! Again, I knew I had to leave. I was not numb any longer. I could not keep living like this. That song had given me hope, and it was growing daily. Leaving his house for the last time was hard. I left without shoes in the middle of the night in a rainstorm. But because of that choice, God could finally start to calm the storm inside of me. A few weeks later, I called Jenny on the phone for the very first time. I told her that I had left for good. She asked me what my plan was. I told her I'd call her back when I figured it out.

When I did, I called her Mom. I guess it's weird to call someone Mom whom you've never met before, but it felt right. As soon as the words were out of my mouth, I was embarrassed, but she laughed and said, "God told me I would have daughters one day." We continued to talk and build a relationship. One day she asked me if I wanted to come home.

On May 27, 2010, I got on a plane to fly to California and to call people "family" that I had never met before and move into a house I had never seen. Courage House. My home. God fulfilled the little-girl prayer of my heart that I would be rescued, have a new family, and a place to sleep where no one came into my bedroom late at night.

However, I have found so much more. I have found freedom and hope and a future. I have found that long before time began, I was created on purpose for a purpose—all because people simply believed in me and called me family. All because of one woman's fight for her identity and destiny; all because she had the courage to be and do all God created her to. All because she decided to be a voice for the voiceless, build them homes, and call them family. Jenny, my mom, gave me permission to speak. Now I can help other girls discover their identity and fulfill their destiny.

This is why you cannot quit. Someone is praying a prayer and waiting on God, and He is waiting on you.

I will ask you one last time,

Do you have the courage to be you?

EPILOGUE

⁓

*M*y family was not consulted when I began this journey of purpose. I probably should have talked to them, but it never occurred to me to consider the implications of praying this prayer: *"God, use me and our family to change the world—one individual at a time."*

I have loved and love being a wife, and I have loved and love being a mom of boys. I would give my life, time, and last dime to the men in my life. My longing to matter does not diminish these roles. I believe I am a better wife and mother because of this journey.

Since this writing, there have been hundreds of girls who have called Courage House home and have called me Mom. Each is my daughter. Some are from the United States, and some are from Tanzania, Africa. But sadly, because of a lack of space, we say no to more girls than we are able to help.

When each girl arrives at Courage House, I tell them the story I have told you through the pages of this book. They are also told that before time began, they were created on purpose for a purpose, that God imagined them, planned them, and that He has something for them to do that only they can do; if they do not do it, it will never be done.

I tell each of them that although I cannot wipe away or even begin to explain the *why* of their past, I do promise them that we will walk with them into their future. I promise each child we will be there when the nightmares and flashbacks come. We will love them until they learn to love themselves. We will call them family. They will always have a home. And for those who have had to go . . . we pray that they will come back home.

A blessing from your Creator:

> *Get up! Be bright! Stop playing small, for I have covered you with the bright light of my love, and my splendor shoots forth light beams from you and upon you. Though the world is a dark place, you bring the brightness of my love. I have made you to be bright so others will be drawn to you. My glory is literally on you. Stand. Rise. Be seen. Do not shrink from your destiny. You reflect my heart. Do not fear the darkness; it should fear you.*

Go now. Someone is waiting for you to have the courage to be you.

NOTES

1   Henri Nouwen, Parting Words: *A Conversation with Henri Nouwen,* a reprint of Sacred Journey Classics in The Journal of Fellowship in Prayer, 2000.

2   Crowe, Cameron. 1996. Jerry Maguire. United States: TriStar Pictures.

3   "Truth," Merriam-Webster's Dictionary, https://www.merriam-webster.com/dictionary/truth.

4   "Faith," Dictionary.com, https://www.dictionary.com/browse/faith.

5   "Do You Know the Health Risks of Being Overweight?" US Department of Health and Human Services, National Institutes of Health, updated October 2007, http://www.nwtcc.com/assets/obesity.pdf.

6   "Emotions," Dictionary.com, https://www.dictionary.com/browse/emotion.

7   Tom Rath, *StrengthsFinder 2.0* (New York, NY: Gallup Press, 2007).

8   The Enneagram Institute: Your Basic Personality Type, https://www.enneagraminstitute.com/how-the-enneagram-system-works. Accessed June 29, 2023.

9   U.S. Army Soldier's Creed, https://www.army.mil/values/soldiers.html.

10   Bruce Wilkinson, David Kopp, and Heather Kopp, *The Dream Giver* (Colorado Springs, CO: Multnomah Books, 2003).

11 "Passion," Merriam-Webster's, https://www.merriam-webster.com/dictionary/passion.

12 "Passion," Dictionary.com, https://www.dictionary.com/browse/passion.

13 This quote is attributed to Eleanor Roosevelt, however there is some possibility the quote came from Mary Schmich in 1997 June 1, Chicago Tribune, "Advice, Like Youth, Probably Just Wasted on the Young" by Mary Schmich, Page 4C, Chicago, Illinois. (ProQuest). https://quoteinvestigator.com/2013/08/09/scare/.

14 Theodore Roosevelt, Speech at the Sorbonne, Paris, April 23, 1910, "It Is Not the Critic Who Counts," by Theodore Roosevelt Conservation Partnership staff, January 18, 2011. https://www.trcp.org/2011/01/18/it-is-not-the-critic-who-counts/.

15 Max Lucado, Cure for the Common Life: *Living in Your Sweet Spot* (Nashville: Thomas Nelson, 2005).

ABOUT JENNY WILLIAMSON

*enny Williamson is the Founder and CEO of Courage Worldwide, an international nonprofit organization that builds homes for children recovered from sex trafficking around the world. The homes are called Courage Houses. Jenny works tirelessly to see children recovered from this evil be provided with a safe, loving home and the resources they need for their unique healing journey so they, too, can hear the life-altering truth that they were created on purpose for a purpose. Courage Houses are places where they can discover their true identity and fulfill their destiny.

For her efforts and impact in the community, Jenny was awarded the FBI Director's Community Leadership Award, the Community Spirit Award by Sacramento's District Attorney, the William Jessup University's prestigious Community Impact Award, the L'Oreal Women of Worth Award, the George H. W. Bush Point of Light Award for individuals who demonstrate the transformative power of service and who drive significant and sustained impact through their everyday actions and words that light the path for others to do the same, and she was invited to be part of the California Attorney General's Working Group on human trafficking. She was also part of Shared Hope International's Practitioners Working Group for their National Colloquium meeting in Washington, D.C., and is a member of the Abolition International Shelter Association's advisory board.

As a professionally trained life coach and results-driven business leader, Jenny is known for her contagious energy, her motivational speeches, and her passion for changing the world. She is an international speaker and has a passion for courageously being and doing all God created her for and absolutely refuses to settle for less. She encourages everyone she meets to do the same.

Jenny and her family live in Northern Nevada, where she also acts as the chief financial officer of their family business. To book Jenny to speak at your next event, complete the speaker request form at jennytwilliamson.com. You can also follow Jenny on Facebook, Instagram, or LinkedIn.

For more information on the organization Jenny founded or to be one of the million somebodies who will build one thousand homes in one hundred countries in ten years so hundreds of thousands of children can be rescued from the evil of sex trafficking, visit courageworldwide.org.

facebook.com/
jenny.t.williamson

@jennytwilliamson

linkedin.com/in/
jennytwilliamson/

jennytwilliamson.com

ABOUT COURAGE WORLDWIDE

Changing the World One Individual at a Time

*C*ourage Worldwide is committed to providing safe houses and resources for child victims of sex trafficking so they can reach their full potential.

We believe every child survivor should have the support necessary to begin their journey of hope and healing.

It is our passion to both expand our current homes *and* build a Courage House in every city around the world that needs one to bring more girls home. With your help, we can accomplish this goal, working together to provide the safety and resources these survivors need to begin their journey of hope and healing.

To learn more, volunteer, or make a tax-deductible donation, visit www. courageworldwide.org or scan the QR code below.

Get involved today!

OTHER BOOKS BY JENNY WILLIAMSON

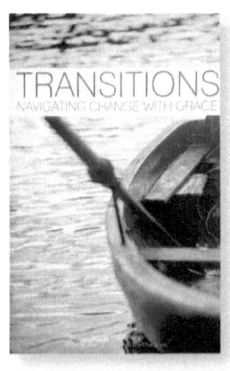

Transitions
Navigating Change with Grace

Change is inevitable. It's what you do with change that matters. In *Transitions*, Jenny Williamson shares openly how God used her own difficult transitions to move her out of her comfort zone to the unknown—a place where destinies are found that change the course of history. Transitions are not easy, but they are necessary if you are ever to do what you have been created to do. You can navigate change with grace and courage in the midst of the unknown.

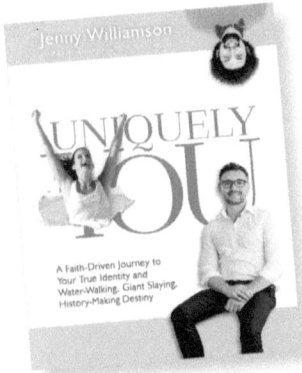

Uniquely You
A 10-week Faith-Driven Journey to Your True Identity and Water-Walking, Giant-Slaying, History-Making Destiny

Join Jenny Williamson as she walks you through a very intentional journey of purpose and courage. Discover your true identity and destiny as you walk step by step through a journey of self-discovery and honest assessment. Hundreds of men and women have taken this challenge and been changed. You can be changed, too! This interactive workbook contains ten weeks of exercises, assessments, and special messages from Jenny, which are accessible on your computer or mobile device. This study is perfect for men or women and can be done in small groups (recommended) or as an individual.

—————— Available at Amazon & Barnes & Noble ——————

www.ingramcontent.com/pod-product-compliance
Lightning Source LLC
Chambersburg PA
CBHW020236130626
46549CB00005B/1923